Spey Casting

Dean River Afternoon by Greg Pearson

Spey Casting

SIMON GAWESWORTH

STACKPOLE BOOKS

Published by
STACKPOLE BOOKS
5067 Ritter Road
Mechanicsburg, PA 17055
www.stackpolebooks.com

Printed in China

First edition

10 9 8 7 6 5 4 3 2 1

Photographs by Scott Nelson
Illustrations by Greg Pearson

Library of Congress Cataloging-in-Publication Data

Gawesworth, Simon.
    Spey casting / Simon Gawesworth.— 1st ed.
        p. cm.
    Includes index.
    ISBN 0-8117-0104-2; 0-8117-0129-8 (special limited edition)
    1. Spey casting. I. Title.
SH454.25 .G38 2004
799.12'4—dc22
                                    2003025414

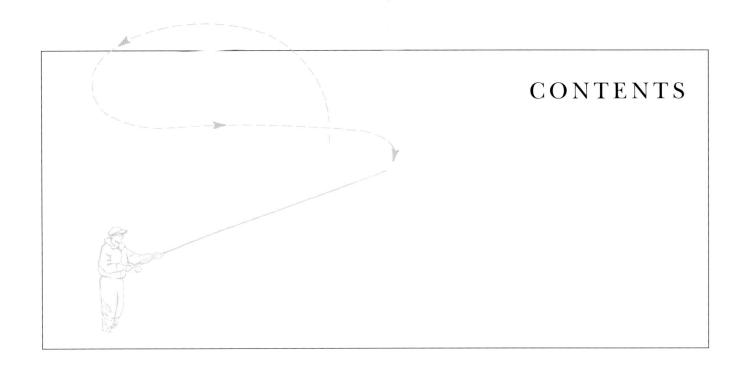

CONTENTS

For my dad—my mentor
For the noble Salmon—my respect
For Susan, Chloe, and Tristan—my universe

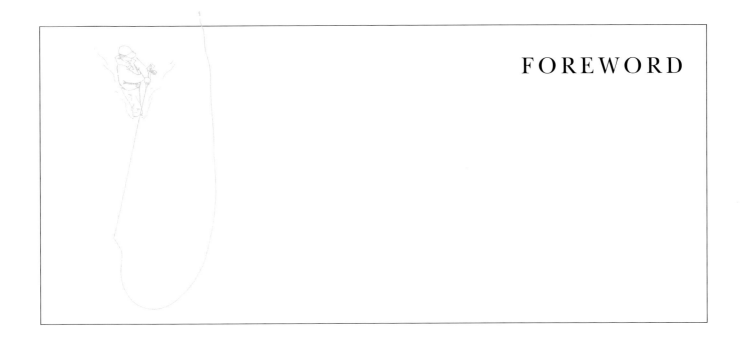

There was a time not so long ago when North Americans saw the double-handed rods used by Europeans as an unfailing sign of their backwardness, their lack of evolution as anglers. The view was that the single-handed rod was so much less work, especially with the new materials available, that to go on with the double-hander was ignorant. Lee Wulff spoke for us all when he stated, "Rods over twelve-and-a-half feet are becoming relics now, used for sentiment." This view even affected the practice of Europeans who took up single-handed rods on their salmon rivers in surprising numbers. Then, not much more than a decade ago, the double-handed rod emerged from the shadows, this time with a vengeance. On both sides of the Atlantic, anglers were cutting up and splicing perfectly good lines to find more efficient alternatives to the usual double tapers, and the two-handed rod came to be known, to the dismay of its inventors, as the spey rod. What brought this on? First, anglers discovered that for covering moving water, the double-handed rod is much less work than the single-hander. The mingling of practices may well have occurred on the new anadromous fisheries in far-flung parts of the world like the Kola Peninsula of Russia and Tierra del Fuego. Here, with big rivers and big fish, the single-handers could look upon the two-handers, shoulder to shoulder, and see their advantages. (I remember arriving at the Ponoi River in Russia, the highest volume salmon river in the world, and being told by the guides that the Brits with the double-handers were rather dominating things.) While the single-hander is laboriously stripping running line back to the head of his shooting taper, the double hander has moved downstream, cast again, and resumed fishing in less time than it takes to tell it. Anyone fishing a single-handed rod down a long run behind a competent spey caster experiences the steady pulling away of his companion until the time comes when, having fished through, the spey caster is pulling up behind him. Where water coverage matters, spey casting offers real advantages in catching fish; where fish are pooled up as with some chinook fishing, it probably makes little difference, and its usefulness in still water remains to be seen. Today, efficient water coverage in rivers can be paramount. In very cold conditions, the spey caster avoids the cold, blue hands that accompany constant line handling. Finally, in fishing big rivers for big fish, bites can be few and far between; it can't hurt that the complexity and beauty of spey casting produces pleasure in itself or that the learning never quite comes to an end.

Without a doubt, the rediscovery of the two-handed rod took on all the appearances of a fad, with explanatory article after explanatory article appearing in the angling press, websites launched, and chat rooms inaugurated. English, Scandinavian, and North American positions about proper casting hardened. Rod and line designs arose and disappeared with astounding speed. Americans, late on the scene, brought such technical acuity to the tackle that in a short time American rods were the commonest around the world. Ten-year-old graphite two-handers became the subject of nostalgia. As ever, agreement on proper actions is hard to find, thus multiplying niches for rod builders. But much has been purposeful, and we may be approaching a tackle plateau, where the only real remaining breakthrough lies in price lowering in the wake of diminished research and development.

Throughout this period, various authorities have appeared on the scene, giving clinics, advising manufacturers, and writing books. Some good came from all of them, but for the end-user, the fisherman, it seemed a Babel of warring voices. The time had arrived for the definitive book on spey casting. This is it.

Simon Gawesworth brings an extraordinary amount of benefits to the task, perhaps least of which is that he is a champion tournament caster. He is a widely experienced angler with remarkably few prejudices about the quarry. From the tiny trout of Normandy to the Atlantic salmon of Russia, to the bounty of American public waters, Gawesworth has found unjaded pleasure in the original rewards of angling. He has studied the physics of spey casting with an eye to removing the voodoo that confuses students and subjected his theory to practice in innumerable casting schools. He owns a patient amiability, which, combined with extraordinary powers of observation, enables him to instruct clearly without enlarging the learner's inhibitions. He has avoided the zealotry of a particular school of casting and, for someone of such long experience, is remarkably free of fixed ideas. The new casts that have resulted from the resurgence of two-handed rods—sometimes in fisheries where they were previously unknown—are enthusiastically examined by Gawesworth. He has a capacity for encouragement, clear explanation, humorous and helpful analogies, homilies, and witticisms—all with the purpose of teaching and improving spey casting. While his goal is to get the spey caster up and running and back to his river, he is well aware that the refinements and aesthetics of this activity can contribute to pleasure in angling.

It is our good fortune that he writes as well and as clearly as he does: No one else could have done it.

Thomas McGuane
McLeod, Montana
December 2003

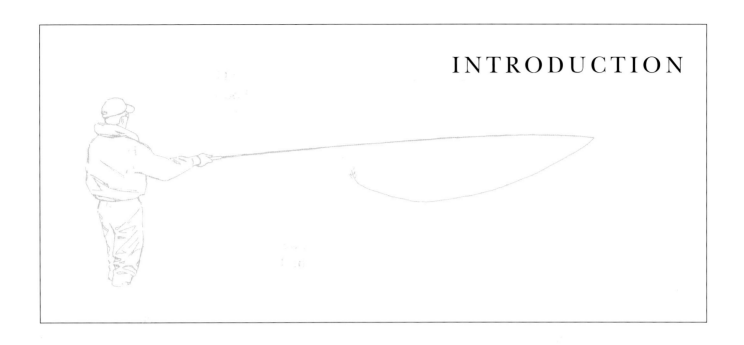

INTRODUCTION

Spey casting is a fly-casting technique that developed in Scotland in the mid-1800s, probably on the river Spey—one of Scotland's premier salmon rivers. What is peculiar about spey casting is that it is a form of casting that has no backcast as such. When you see the river Spey, you will understand why this style of casting evolved on such a river. The Spey is a wide, powerful river. It is too fast to be able to wade out far enough to make space for an overhead cast and rarely are there nice gravel bars on which you can fish from. Also, nks are lined with trees that run right down to er's edge. All in all this is a river that needs spey casting to be able to catch the Atlantic salmon that run there.

The first two-handed salmon rods that were built for spey casting and these big rivers were heavy and long. Some were made of greenheart—a heavy wood imported from British Guyana. Some were made of split cane; some even had two layers of split cane one on top of the other. There was even a series of rods that had two layers of split cane *and* a steel shaft going up the middle! A small rod in those days was 15 feet long and frequently anglers used rods up to 20 and 22 foot. It was thought that the weight and length of these rods would help the caster get a line out there. Thank goodness for the introduction of carbon fiber and lightweight rods!

Despite the tackle that was used, it didn't seem to put people off going fly fishing for salmon, and soon spey casting became de rigueur in salmon fishing circles. It was the "in" thing, the fashionable way of fly fishing. The interest and growth in Britain and Europe became so popular that anyone going salmon fishing was going to use a two-handed rod—not necessarily for spey casting, but at least a two-handed rod. That trend still exists today in Europe. In the United States, it is the latest buzz and is the fastest-growing side of fly casting. People are finding out that it is a jolly effective way of fishing as well as being quite fun. With the recent interest in spey casting, rod manufacturers are making smaller and lighter rods to appeal to the trout angler—so the growth continues. With that growth comes a thirst for knowledge and information, hence this book.

In attempting to write this book on spey casting, I have opened up the proverbial can of worms. This has been a four-year venture in my life trying to find the words that will turn someone into a competent spey caster. It is not really possible—learning how to spey cast through words, photos, and illustrations. There is no doubt that to truly master any form of spey casting, a direct, one-to-one lesson with an expert instructor is the *only* way to succeed. Videos do help; these are moving images where the viewer can see what everything *should* look like, though success comes down to the interpretation of the viewer and whether they can remember what they watched last week! Videos also don't tell the caster what they did wrong. A book is not the ideal medium for learning. It is a way of giving an understanding on

The author fishing the river Spey at Carron and Laggan, one of the finest and most enjoyable salmon rivers in the world to fish and birthplace of the spey casts.

the principles, dynamics, and physics of the cast, but do not expect to master this tricky little group of casts with the memory of the words written forthcoming. Muscle memory is more important. Note that I have written the instructions for each cast for the right-handed caster. For left-handed casting, use the opposite hand and feet positions.

As you will see in the forthcoming chapters, spey casting is not limited to the salmon or steelhead angler and to the big 15- to 18-foot rods that spey casting has traditionally been associated with. This book has been written with the ordinary fly caster in mind, whether a trout, striped bass, salmon, or steelhead fly fisher. Whatever your quarry, at some stage there will be obstructions behind you and about the only way to get a fly out in this situation is with a spey cast.

I hope this book encourages many casters to take up spey casting for the first time, maybe even help a few casters get a better technique and understanding of what they are trying to do. Above all, though, I just want to share some of the knowledge and experiences I have gained over the years with like-minded spey junkies and hope that I get the chance to compare styles and techniques with every one of them!

Idaho Falls
September 2003

CHAPTER 1

What Is Spey Casting?

The main difference between spey casting and regular overhead casting is that there isn't a backcast where the fly goes behind the caster. The most obvious use, therefore, is when there are obstructions behind the fly caster that prevent an overhead cast from being used.

There are other reasons to use the spey casts, though. There is no doubt that the spey casts, once mastered, use much less effort to pick up a line and change direction than the overhead cast. They are also a quicker way to change direction, meaning more time is spent with the fly in the water fishing. Spey casting is also safer, and you get fewer wind knots! All in all, they are extremely useful casts to learn and, as a Scottish ghillie told me, once you have learned how to spey cast, you will never use the overhead cast again (for across and down fishing on a river!).

Spey casting is wonderful! The skill, timing, and moves that make up a spey cast are beautiful to watch and extremely satisfying to perform. It is more akin to art, or poetry, than a way to get a hook into a river. It is, however, all too easy to get frustrated with the learning process and declare to your casting instructor "my casting doesn't look like yours." Patience and practice are the virtues of a spey caster. It requires perfect timing and a feel for the line that does not develop overnight—no matter how good an overhead caster you are.

It is a great fallacy that the spey casts are only for the two-handed fly rods, as there are many fishing situations where a caster with a single-handed rod cannot use the overhead cast. Later on in the book, I will address the possibilities that the spey cast can open up for the single-handed rod. I shall refer to two-handed fly rods in this book as just that, two-handed rods. In the States, where spey casting is really taking off and becoming an essential part of the fly caster's armory, the two-handed rod is referred to as a "spey rod." This is misleading, as one can overhead-cast these "spey rods" as well as spey-cast them.

Many anglers know of the roll cast and use this when there is an obstacle in the way. Indeed, the roll cast is one in the family of spey casts, along with five other relatives: the switch cast, the single spey, the double spey, the snake roll and the snap T. Each of these casts, their applications, how to perform them, and typical common faults is addressed throughout this book, as well as some of the less regular spey casts.

Anyone learning to spey cast needs to recognize the initial three measures of success. The first is, "Did I avoid hooking myself?" After that, "Did I avoid hooking the trees behind me?" And finally, "Did the fly get out into the river roughly where I wanted it to go and where it could catch a fish?" It is not necessary to perfect and master the spey casts in order to catch fish. As long as the cast is getting the fly out there, the cast is working.

All the spey casts can be broken down into one of two groups: splash and go or waterborne anchor. This will give you an understanding of the importance of the timing of the forward cast with each cast. The splash and go casts all have a backstroke that is airborne, that falls to the water, and the forward cast starts the *instant* the line tip splashes the water. The waterborne anchor casts have a backcast that stays on the water, so there is no instantaneous requirement to start the forward cast. Timing depends on how big the belly is and how far back it will travel. With these casts, you must wait until the belly stops moving backwards before starting the forward stroke.

The process of learning to spey cast, then, follows distinct steps: To begin with, you are quite happy in giving the subject mild attention and satisfied with the occasional success. But once you become interested in spey casting, you want to learn more. You begin to ask, "How far can I cast?" If you want to cast farther and better, you'll need to become more intent on learning. Anyone serious about the sport needs to understand the hows and whys of spey casting. Take a lesson from a professionally qualified instructor and spend time practicing to master the cast. You may become passionate, spending as much time as you can getting your technique right. You now want to know, "What does my casting look like?" You may become so interested in casting beautifully that catching a fish almost becomes a distraction.

Later on in this book I go into a little detail on rods and the different actions available. This is definitely one of the biggest factors influencing a casting style and should not be overlooked. The techniques I use and talk about are all based on the faster action rods—performance rods. The softer, more classic spey rods work very well with the classic spey casting techniques—the big figure-eight movements and swoops of the rod, the smooth arm drive on the forward cast and the wider stroke of the final delivery. The modern style of spey casting has come about though the development of lighter and faster action rods—rods that do not load up with the classic style of spey casting. While this fast action rod is not for everybody, it is the type of rod that will achieve the longest casts—in competent hands.

There are many different styles of spey casting. This book is not going to show you *the* way to spey cast. This is just an interpretation of the techniques that have worked for me, both as a caster and as an instructor. Some people will read this book and decide they do it differently. Others will find that my techniques don't work for them or their tackle. Ultimately, most casters will settle into a style of their own and as long as the fly gets to the fish, it doesn't really matter what the cast looks like.

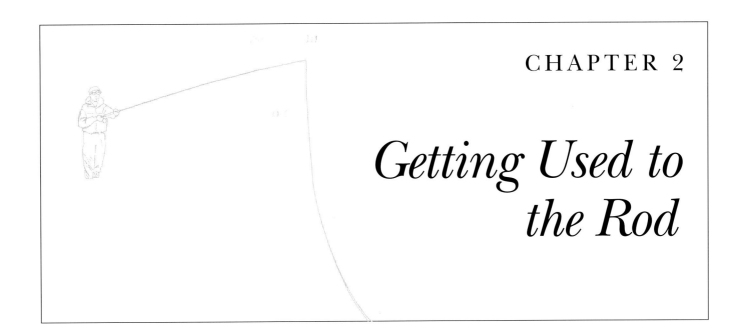

CHAPTER 2

Getting Used to the Rod

Most casters who convert from a single-handed rod to a two-handed rod have three problems. The first is that the right hand (for a right-handed caster) has muscle memory. No matter how hard a beginner spey caster tries to control the upper hand, it wants to cast as it always has. For example, when making a backcast with a single-handed rod, you lift and accelerate and end the backcast with a short positive stop. Do this while making a spey cast with a spey rod and you will immediately send your backcast into the nearest bush behind you. It takes a lot of concentration to make the backcast with a dead rod and steer the line into position, rather than power it into position.

Casters of single-handed rods find it is quite alien for the bottom hand to do any work at all. Sure, if you are double hauling with a single-handed rod, the left hand is doing some work, but not with the rod directly. Now, with a two-handed rod, you have to get the feel of applying as much power with the bottom hand as with the top hand—a 50/50 ratio.

Finally, almost everyone who picks up a 14- or 15-foot spey rod to learn with is awed by its size. "It is so long and so much heavier than I am used to," is the common response. You might think the effort required to cast these longer, heavier rods is going to be tenfold the effort needed to cast a single-handed rod. In fact, the length of the rod works in your favor, giving you a tremendously long lever. Since the tip speed generated by this long lever is fantastic and transmits directly to the line, you need to use less power to achieve the same distance, which is why we're attracted to the two-handed rods in the first place.

The problem is that the brain has a tough time concentrating on more than one thing at a time. So, if your mind is focused on the moves of the spey cast, muscle memory from the single-handed rod takes over and makes it hard to make a good cast. For this reason alone, casting with your wrong hand is a great teaching aid as there is no muscle memory to overcome, and as a result, the cast is actually easier to learn.

Only time and practice can make the two-handed rod seem comfortable and the fine, precise tool that it is.

CHAPTER 3

Grip and Stance

The most important thing to realize about the way you grip the rod and the stance you use is that you want to be comfortable and balanced. Hold the rod with a grip that helps you stay relaxed and stand in a position that easily allows you to be safe, whatever current and riverbed you are going to come across. Sometimes you'll stand with the right foot forward and sometimes the left foot forward—safety is your number one priority with stance. After that, there are a few tips that can help you get a better casting foundation.

GRIP

With the two-handed salmon rod, two factors determine your grip position—the point of balance of the rod (controlled by the weight of the reel) and the length of the cork handle (and your arms) on the rod. Hold the rod with your hands as far apart as is comfortable. The reason this works so well for me is that I tend to use both arms in the power application of the forward cast. As the rod is driven forward, the upper hand snaps the rod tip out and, at the same moment, the lower hand tugs the rod butt back toward me—I call this "push-me-pull-you." The amount of power used by both hands should be roughly equal—in other words, the lower hand tugs back just as hard as the upper arm snaps forward.

One very good pointer as to whether you are using both arms on the power stroke, or just driving

with the upper arm (which accounts for about 90 percent of spey casters initially converting from the single-handed rod), is how the rod has finished at the end of the forward cast. If done correctly, the rod butt should lie along the forearm and upper arm with the butt cap close to the upper hand's armpit. All too often casters finish with the lower arm stuck out a foot or two from the body, proving conclusively that the lower arm has not contributed anything to the power stroke.

To enable you to get the most from the power stroke, you do need to have a wide grip, and your arm length will effect how far up the rod you hold it. The easiest way to find this position for right-handed casters is to hold the rod very loosely in your right hand at an arm's length. (Left-handed casters use your left hand.) Slide the rod through your right hand until the butt grip nestles comfortably under your right armpit. Where your right hand is holding the rod is the best place to grip it for casting efficiency. The lower hand wants to rest comfortably at the lower end of the butt grip.

The one thing that could change this rod grip position is the weight of the reel. More important than your holding the rod with a wide grip is that you hold the very point of balance with your upper hand on the rod. This helps you cast with the least amount of effort. Why use more energy than you have to? You will use much less effort to cast the rod

The correct rod finishing position at the end of the forward stroke. Note how the rod butt lies along the upper forearm, indicating that the bottom hand has been used to good effect. See also how wide the grip is and how the rod butt nestles into the armpit.

by holding the rod with your upper hand directly on the balance point of the rod, than if you hold the rod far away from this balance point. (If your reel choice is correct, this will be in the same place as mentioned in the previous paragraph). The farther away from the balance point you hold the rod, the more work you have to do, and the more strain you put on your muscles and tendons.

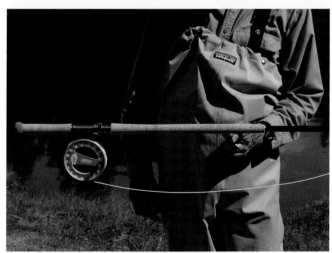

A good balance point. Where the rod balances on the finger is where the upper hand should grip the rod.

Incorrect rod finishing position. The rod has finished away from the forearm, indicating that little or no bottom hand has been used as part of the forward cast.

Here the reel choice is too light for the rod and the point of balance too far up the rod. You need to hold the rod where the finger balances or you will quickly become fatigued.

Right hand up, left foot forward is a good stance where it is safe to do so. This allows the caster to transfer his full body weight during the back and forward stroke and have full hip, knee, and ankle rotation.

STANCE

Stance, as with grip, should be comfortable (and safe). For the very best and most efficient casting, much of the power comes through the body and in the way you transfer your body weight and rotate your body. Just like any other sport involving propelling an object for distance (golf, cricket, and baseball), the way you move your body contributes to the outcome of the cast. Most casts start with

some body movement as far down as the ankles, traveling through the knees and hips and right up to the shoulders as you rotate through some of the backstrokes. Also, there is a very important weight transference from one foot to the other as you rock back slightly and then forward slightly on the final delivery (not when you are wading chest deep in a powerful current, though).

All this is possible with the correct stance and really adds distance and reduces effort at the same time. As in the sports mentioned earlier (golf, cricket, and baseball), the most efficient stance is with the opposite foot to hand. A right-hand-up caster should stand with the left foot forward and the left-hand-up caster should stand with the right

foot forward. No golfer, cricketer, or baseball player would stand with his right foot forward when hitting right handed and fly casting follows the same body dynamics.

In theory this is fine, but with some casts like the single spey, this means rotating your body against the natural stance to start the cast. Although initially uncomfortable, when you have started the backstroke and are in the set-up position for the all important forward cast, the body will regain its natural position and be comfortable and powerful throughout the forward stroke.

However, bear in mind that when you are wading you are going to have rocks, weed beds, and deep holes to negotiate—all of which might make it

Left hand up, right foot forward, as with the other hand up, is the best stance for maximum performance where it is safe to do so.

impossible to stand in the correct casting stance. Safety should be your number one concern.

I have heard a number of spey casters explain that casting with the right foot forward and the right hand up prevents back ache, or prevents too much body rotation—this works for some casters and seems to be quite comfortable for them. However, to get the maximum performance from your ability and tackle, the opposite foot usually will work better.

CHAPTER 4

The Overhead Cast

The overhead cast is not a spey cast, but there are more and more fly fishermen using the overhead cast with two-handed rods, particularly in the United States, so it is worth a mention here. There are a number of advantages that the overhead cast has over the spey cast and in certain fishing situations that make this a valuable cast to know.

Years ago when I used to compete in tournament casting in the United Kingdom, tournaments consisted of eleven events—a mixture of accuracy and distance with the fly rod, fixed spool reel, and multiplier reel. There were a few two-handed events, all distance, and in particular one that I seemed to do well at—the two-handed fly rod distance event.

The rods in tournament casting have to be seen to be believed. Seventeen feet long, poker stiff, with the butt section thick enough to grip with no cork— just the bare blank—and a tip diameter about as thick as a little finger. The lines used to load these rods were extremely heavy, weighing over $^{1}/_{4}$ pound—around 1850 grains. In the modern fly-line world a 15-weight line weighs 550 grains at 30 feet; this will give you some idea of how heavy the tournament lines were and how stiff the rods needed to be. The lines were about 17 meters long and attached to a very thin monofilament shooting line. We used a shock section of about 25-pound breaking strain— just long enough to ensure there was no light running line in the rod rings—and then we attached this to a 10-pound monofilament as the shooting line. Being so light, the 10-pound test material had virtually no drag and gave us good distances.

I used to love this event and did pretty well, winning the British Championships many years running and setting distance records in the United Kingdom that still stand today. My longest tournament cast was 88 meters (about 286 feet), though my personal best was a 94-meter cast (around 308 feet) I made in practice at the West of England tournament casting club. This, of course, proves nothing and the tackle has nothing to do with fishing gear, but it was one of the contributing factors that really piqued my interest in the two-handed rod, and ultimately in spey casting.

At age 14 the author won his first casting competition in Bodmin, Cornwall, England.

A good forward loop should unroll in the air, parallel to the water, remaining quite narrow with a wedge-shaped front end instead of a rounded nose.

Whether using an overhead cast in tournaments or fishing, there are certain principles that have to be understood to get a good cast. As with the single-handed rod, when using a two-handed rod a narrow, tight loop is desirable, and this is achieved by keeping the rod tip traveling in a straight line throughout the casting stroke. The length of the stroke contributes to its acceleration—the longer the stroke, the longer the acceleration and the greater speed the rod will have at the end of the stroke. Thus, in tournament casting, you start the backcast with a

steady acceleration, stopping the rod crisply to create a tight loop, then drifting the rod back with the momentum of the backcast until the rod is mostly horizontal and the lower hand is pushed away from your chest. As the forward cast starts, the rod accelerates over this great length, and then the bottom hand snaps the rod butt toward your body (at the same time the top hand snaps forward), generating fantastic speed and, of course, great distances. Good distance is achieved with this technique, whether you are fishing or tournament casting. The reason that you cannot use this style of casting for fishing is that you have a fly on and you will probably hook the grass behind you when drifting your rod so far back. Also, with too tight a loop, you will frequently tangle the fly in the line and leader.

For the salmon and steelhead angler, the overhead cast is easier to learn and to master than the more complex spey casts. It is a better cast to use when fishing short shooting heads of 30 to 40 feet or so, and it is a good way to get great distance with a cast, providing there is enough room behind you (and you are not changing direction). Modern shooting heads designed for spey casting are usually around 38 to 45 feet long. This is necessary as the D loop formed by the backcast of the spey cast must have enough line to form the loop and retain an anchor. With too short a line, it is almost impossible to successfully spey cast. So, if you do have a short shooting head of 30 feet or so, the overhead cast gives you one way of getting the line out to the fish.

Using the overhead cast with a two-handed rod is particularly suited for fishing the northeastern coast of the United States. Growing numbers of fly fishermen who fish the surf are using these longer rods to throw big flies a long way for striped bass. The times I have done this, I have been able to cast 160 feet and more with big poppers or baitfish imitations, easily clearing the incoming surf and beating the winds that constantly blow on the coast. A word of warning though: With so much running line dangling around your feet and being blown about in the wind, constantly tangling and hooking shrub and scrub on the ground, a stripping basket is a vital purchase for the overhead caster combing the surf line.

There are a good number of spey casters, too, who use the spey cast to change direction in a river, and then finish off with an overhead cast to get distance. For some anglers, this is an effective way to fish fast sinking tips or heavy flies. Of course, the successful spey caster doesn't need an extra cast to finish off the spey cast, as the spey cast will do this effectively, whatever size fly or sink tip.

Last, and by no means least, the overhead cast is a way of getting these crazy two-handed rods to cast a long line—if you don't have the knowledge or ability to spey cast.

So, there are legitimate reasons for overhead casting the wonderful two-handed rod. However, an old ghillie once told me, "Once you learn to spey cast, you will never need or want to overhead cast again." That was sound advice and I am now so comfortable in my spey casting that I never do anything other

Using a two-handed rod to fly-fish the surf is becoming very popular on the East Coast of the United States. The rod length helps throw a long line out over the incoming surf. Here Monomy guide, Randy Jones, cradles a nice striper caught on a two-handed rod. *Photo courtesy of Jay and Joyce Horton.*

than spey cast in these fishing situations, regardless of whether there is room behind me or not.

There is not much difference in overhead casting a two-handed rod than a single handed rod—in technique anyway. The rod is longer, so it can generate much more tip speed and, therefore, more distance than the shorter single-handed rod. Also, the rods can take a heavier line to load them (though with 5-weight spey rods available now, this isn't quite as true as it used to be). The real difference lies in that you use two hands to hold the rod, instead of one. The successful overhead caster uses both hands together on a power stroke.

The overhead cast starts with the line washed tight
and the rod pointing straight down the line and low to
the water.

Start the backcast by lifting the rod with a smooth acceleration. Both hands lift together, the bottom hand supporting the top, as you would lift a shotgun, rather than lifting the upper hand and pushing the lower hand away.

As the rod reaches about 11 o'clock, it is well flexed and still accelerating. At this point you power the backstroke with a short, hard jab out with the bottom hand and, at the same time, a short, hard flick with the upper hand. The rod needs to come to a definite, positive stop.

At the end of the backcast, the rod is back to about 1 o'clock. For maximum distance (caster's skill and room behind permitting), the rod should start to drift back with the backcast to a horizontal position, somewhere near 2 o'clock. Note that the bottom hand is slightly away from the body.

Like the front loop, the back loop should be tight, small, and traveling parallel to the water. The rod tip remains completely still while the back loop is unrolling (unless you are imparting drift).

The forward cast starts with a smooth acceleration, similar to the backcast, loading the rod against the back loop. It is very important that the rod does not start forward with any tilt. Compare this photo to the one on the next page and you will see that both of the caster's hands have moved forward without tilting the rod. This is the only way to get a full load on the rod. Then the rod tilts through the power stroke and finishes as on the next page.

The rod tip should travel horizontally to keep a tight front loop; do not let it roll forward in an arc, as this will give you sloppy loops. In this photo, the rod has extended forward as far as possible and the bottom hand is pulling the butt of the rod toward the caster's body—the late tilt.

As the rod reaches the extension of the drive, the upper hand fires the rod forward, stopping quite high to keep the loop small and tight above the water, while the lower hand tugs the butt end of the rod back to you. With a correct stroke such as this, the bottom hand has snapped the rod butt close to the upper forearm. Both movements happen simultaneously with equal amounts of power.

While the forward cast goes out, the forward loop should unroll completely above the water with enough speed to shoot the line before any of the fly line lands on the water.

There are very few times that you need to use a false cast with a two-handed rod, and shooting line is usually achieved with a single cast, maybe one false cast at the most, to get the head out to the rod tip, then the final cast to shoot it out the huge distances these rods are capable of. This makes the long lever of these two-handed rods very efficient, even for just the simple overhead cast.

CHAPTER 5

The Basic Principles

Regardless of the type of spey cast, there are three fundamental principles to get right. This also means that there are only three things that can go wrong with the cast (assuming the caster is using the correct hand for the wind conditions), but there are numerous causes for the three mistakes!

Some of what follows may be a bit overwhelming. Don't give up—make your way through the principles. Remember when you were beginning to fly fish—how confusing it all was? Be patient, persist, take your time, read and reread, take it in a little at a time, and eventually all should become clear.

PRINCIPLE 1—BELLY SIZE

The first principle is the size of the belly—or D loop. For any cast to succeed, and particularly to cast with the minimum effort, the rod has to load. This is relatively easy with an overhead cast—if you are casting with 60 feet of line, having completed the backcast, you'll have 60 feet of line behind the rod to load. However, by the very nature of the spey cast, there is no backcast to help load the rod. This is where the belly size comes in. Take a look at the photos on pages 26 and 27. The first is of an angler attempting to roll cast the line forward. In this example, the caster has a line with a small belly to load the rod. The belly lacks weight and energy and is commonly referred to as a "dead-line roll cast." The resulting cast will be short, fail, or require a lot of effort to get it to roll out in front. The other photo shows an

Basic terminology for all the spey casts

Anchor. The part of the fly line that is lying on the water at the end of the backstroke and before the forward stroke starts. Also called line stick and grip.

Belly. The loop of line that is formed on the backstroke of a spey cast that is *underneath* the rod between the rod tip and the anchor. It is this belly that loads the rod for the forward stroke. Also known as the D loop.

Bloody L. The term I use for an anchor that is lying in an L shape on the water, breaking the 180-degree principle. You can also have a crumpled anchor that is similar to the bloody L, though instead of lying on the water in an L shape, it lies in a crumpled pile of slack.

Point P. The exact spot where the fly line lying on the water comes off the water to form the belly (see the photo on page 25).

The drop. The path of the fly line as it falls to the water on the backcast. If it is correct, the drop is angled slightly to make it possible to time the cast right and avoid too much stick. If the drop is level, the line will fall to the water completely horizontally, making it impossible to get the timing right and ensuring that the cast will fail (see the illustrations on page 28).

When using the overhead cast, you have the entire weight of the fly line behind you on the backcast, which loads the rod and flexes it as the forward cast starts.

angler with a line with a larger belly using a cast called the switch cast or live-line roll cast. With this cast, there is more weight and energy going into loading the rod. Now, as the forward cast starts, the rod flexes back more and fires the forward cast out with a lot more speed. The cast will work and the angler will not need to "hit" it so hard. With a good-size belly like this, you should use something like 70 percent of the power in creating the belly and only 30 percent on the forward stroke—unless shooting line long distances.

Now, this may be in slight contradiction to one of the reasons for spey casting: A cast that has no back-cast and requires no room behind in order to com-plete the cast. Very rarely will you be confronted with a situation where there is *no* backcasting room. Usu-ally you can wade out a little bit and have 5, 10, or even 20 feet (or more) of room behind. In these cases, if you can throw a bigger belly behind, you will outcast and use less effort than the caster who can only form a small belly. Master spey casters can adjust the size of the belly directly to the space behind

Little power is needed on the forward cast because the rod is fully loaded at the end of the backcast.

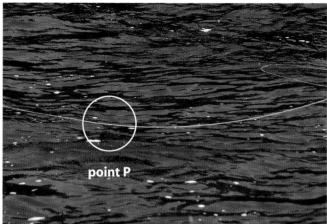

Point P is the exact spot where the belly hanging from the rod tip touches the water.

them—the more space behind, the bigger the belly and the less the effort used on the forward cast. In tight situations, if a small belly is all there is room for, the resulting forward cast will need more power and will not go as far. I call this relationship between the belly size and the amount of power needed for the forward cast to succeed the energy ratio.

Later on, in the chapters dealing with the relevant casts, you will see how to form different sizes of bellies. For now, though, just remember principle 1 is about belly size.

A line with only a small belly to load the rod requires a lot
more power on the forward cast.

The perfect belly is large, has a wedge or **V** shape, and loads the rod much better. This cast requires only the gentlest of forward strokes to succeed.

PRINCIPLE 2—LINE STICK

Line stick is the term used for the fly line that is lying on the water at the start of the forward cast. It is the enemy. The more line that is touching the water the more effort you'll need to break it out of the surface film with the forward stroke. The ideal amount of stick depends on the line length, the caster's reaction time, and the length and action of the rod. Between 2 and 8 feet works well for most casters. However, with a very long line out and a lot of energy in the rear traveling belly, much more stick is needed to anchor the belly, and as much as 20 feet of stick could be right.

It is a difficult thing to get right, but it's critical. If I had to name the most important factor in spey casting, it is to keep the line stick to a minimum.

There are a number of reasons for too much stick. The first is that you have not put enough effort in the backstroke to initially break the surface tension and get the whole fly line and leader out of the water. This is imperative, not only to reduce the line stick, but also to be able to control the size of the belly. Another cause and probably the most common way of creating too much stick is poor timing. When the fly line has been lifted out of the water and is coming back through the air, gravity will pull it down and make it touch the water. At first only the tip of the line will land, but after a quarter of a second the next bit will land, and so on. Basically, the longer you wait, the more line will land on the water—creating more and more stick. Timing is critical. Time it right and you will have

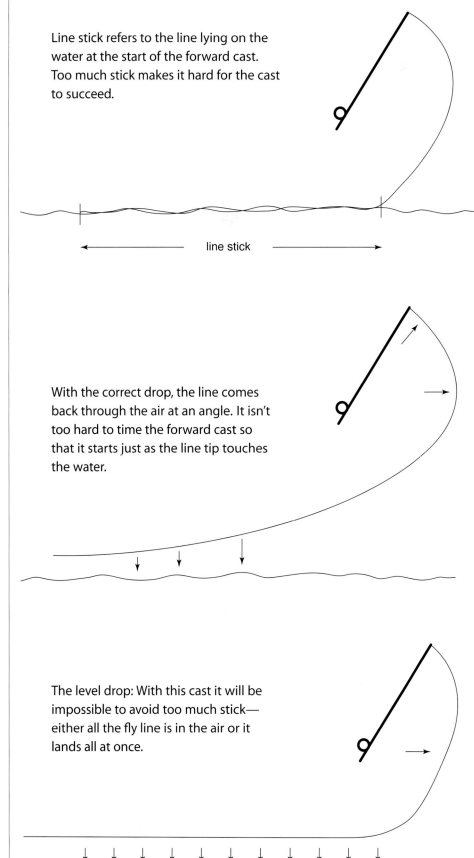

Line stick refers to the line lying on the water at the start of the forward cast. Too much stick makes it hard for the cast to succeed.

line stick

With the correct drop, the line comes back through the air at an angle. It isn't too hard to time the forward cast so that it starts just as the line tip touches the water.

The level drop: With this cast it will be impossible to avoid too much stick—either all the fly line is in the air or it lands all at once.

The trunk starts when your bottom hand pushes away from you on the backcast.

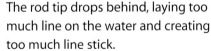

The rod tip drops behind, laying too much line on the water and creating too much line stick.

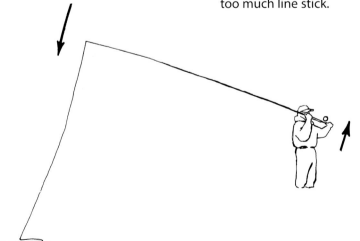

only the first 2 feet of line or so on the water and the line will sail out. Mistime it by even half a second and you may have 20 feet of line on the water, too much for the cast to succeed.

Another cause of too much stick is getting the drop wrong and throwing the line too flat on the backstroke. This is called the level drop. In the bottom diagram on the previous page, you can see that the caster has thrown the line back horizontally. It is either *all* in the air, or *all* on the water—impossible to get the line stick just at the tip of the line.

Perhaps the most common cause of getting the drop wrong is the trunk. This is where the bottom hand pops out on the backcast, pushing the rod away from your chest and causing the tip of the rod to drop and ensuring that the rest of the line will land on the water and create extra stick. For the ideal stopping position, the bottom hand remains fairly tight to the chest and the upper hand level with your ear.

Too much stick is a real problem to solve. There is something that can really help you know if a cast has too much stick or not. As the line leaves the water on the forward cast, the correct amount of anchor will leave the water silently. Too much stick will result in a slurping sound. The louder the slurp, the more stick there is. Hearing the noise, of course, does not cure the problem, but it does let you know that there was too much stick. Next cast, you should be able to adjust your timing or think about the trunk and reduce the slurp, improving the result considerably.

Beginners should use this stopping position on the backcast for all spey casts. Note that the upper hand is about level with the ear and the lower hand close to the chest. More advanced casters can get more acceleration by taking the rod back to 2 o'clock before the start of the forward cast.

PRINCIPLE 3—THE 180-DEGREE PRINCIPLE

An understanding of physics will help you cast better. To understand the 180-degree principle, you'll need to recall some basic physics. Take a catapult, put a stone in the pouch, draw the elastic back, and let go. The stone flies directly away (or 180 degrees) from where the pull came from. A fly rod and line are the same: Bend the fly rod back by pulling the fly line, let the fly line go, and the rod will fire the fly line directly away from the pull. To get the very best and most efficient cast, you should work along such simple, basic physics.

There are three parts to each spey cast that must align on a 180-degree plane:

1. **The Belly.** The belly is the load on the rod. The belly causes the rod to flex backward and loads it for the forward cast. Therefore, the belly wants to be 180 degrees from where the forward cast is going to go. If this is not the case, you end up trying to fight the natural spring of the rod.

2. **The Rod.** The rod fires the forward cast out and, again, is most efficient when the rod is 180 degrees from the target and traveling in a straight line toward the target. Do ensure that at the end of each backcast, the rod is directly opposite where you want to aim the forward cast.

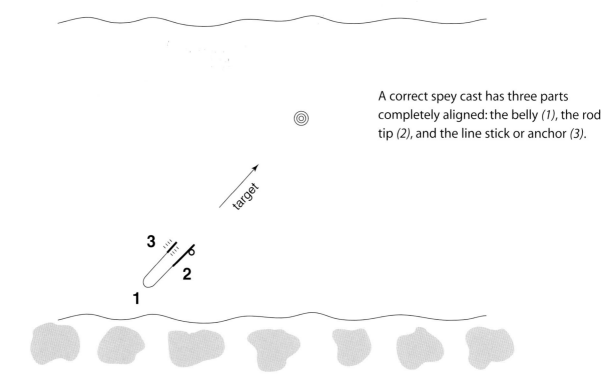

A correct spey cast has three parts completely aligned: the belly *(1)*, the rod tip *(2)*, and the line stick or anchor *(3)*.

Here the fly line lying on the water (the anchor) is straight, taut, directly opposite the rod on the backcast and aligned with the target—perfect!

3. **The Anchor.** Having completed the backstroke of any spey cast, a certain amount of line must touch the water in order to anchor the line and stop it from leaping into the bushes behind. This is the stick mentioned earlier. In a perfect cast, this stick is aligned with the forward cast, tight, and completely straight. Should the stick be off target, have slack in it, or have the bloody L, then the cast loses its potential and will die an inglorious death.

the bloody L

The bloody L can be in an **L** shape like this or just a crumpled heap of slack—either way the forward cast will be ineffective.

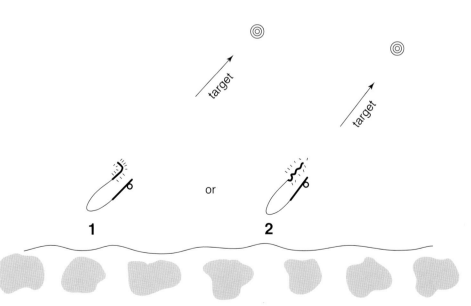

target

target

1   or   **2**

Two types of bloody L can occur and result in a poor cast. *1* is the true bloody L and *2* is another form known as the crumpled anchor. In both cases power is lost on the forward cast as the anchor tries to unravel.

Sometimes it can help to stop a cast in mid-backcast, let the belly fall on the water behind, and see if it is taut and straight with the anchor point and rod opposite the target.

Knowing if you have failed with the 180-degree principle is quite difficult to find out. You can get some idea as the rod doesn't feel loaded, but the cause of this lack of load is the key to solving it and improving your technique. In a cast where the lines of energy are quite a ways off 180 degrees, a form of tailing loop will occur. I call this the collision loop, as it occurs when the caster tries to direct the forward loop contrary to the natural physics of the line's momentum. The result is that the top half of the loop collides with the bottom half. A session spent with a good instructor is invaluable for helping sort out these problems. If you are practicing on your own, the best way of finding out the fault is to look at the line. Freeze everything in mid backstroke and then turn around, look at the line behind, and see if the belly and rod are opposite their target and whether the anchor is aligned, straight, and taut.

CHAPTER 6

The Roll Cast

BACKGROUND

The roll cast is the first and most basic of the casts considered spey casts. It's the founding member of the spey family, if you like. It was the first cast designed to cope with casting a fly out with limited, or no, casting space behind. Many anglers know this cast and use it with single-handed or two-handed rods. Few understand the physics behind the cast and how to improve on what they are doing.

First, the cast is incorrectly named. The name suggests that when one completes the forward stroke of this cast, the line rolls out along the water. This was true in the old days with greenheart, bamboo, split cane, and fiberglass rods. Their characteristic slow, full-flexing action meant that the rod would generally overswing and drop the forward stroke onto the water. I am not a fan of these soft rods because I can cast a lot better, even the humble roll cast, with a more tippy affair. With faster action rods, the roll cast should unroll on the forward cast completely in the air with a nice tight loop (even shooting some line) before landing straight upon the water.

Why use it? Short line length, obstacles behind, no change of direction.
When to use it? Lifting sinking lines and flies up to the surface, straightening out a slack line, and as the final power stroke of the crude spey cast.
Which hand to use? Either!
Group? Waterborne anchor.

There are a couple of key points to remember when doing the roll cast.

1. The most effective roll cast is where the forward stroke is completed *as near as possible to the line* lying on the water in front.

2. Never aim the forward stroke *over* the fly line in front—always roll to the clear side.

3. Always let a belly (D loop) form behind the rod before starting the forward cast. If there is no belly behind the rod, the rod cannot load properly.

An incorrect forward cast rolls along the water with the fly landing last and is the easiest way to get drag when fishing the fly, as well as not casting a long distance.

In a good forward cast, the front loop should unroll completely in the air before landing. This is true for all spey casts and is the only way to cast great distances and be able to shoot line.

You'd have to give a damn good thump to make this forward cast work because there is no belly behind the rod.

HOW TO

It is important to start with a reasonable length of line outside the rod. This will vary, depending on casting ability, the type of line, and the rod used. As a guideline, 30 to 35 feet of line is suitable for a 12-foot rod, 35 to 40 feet for a 13-foot rod, 40 to 45 feet for a 14-foot rod, and 45 to 50 feet for a 15-foot rod. Don't start with too short a length of line, as it can be harder to get the casts right with a short line.

The forward cast is the real factor of a successful roll cast and, in fact, of all the spey casts. Try to think and follow these three words, in this order, to achieve the best result on the forward cast:

1. Body

2. Arm

3. Power

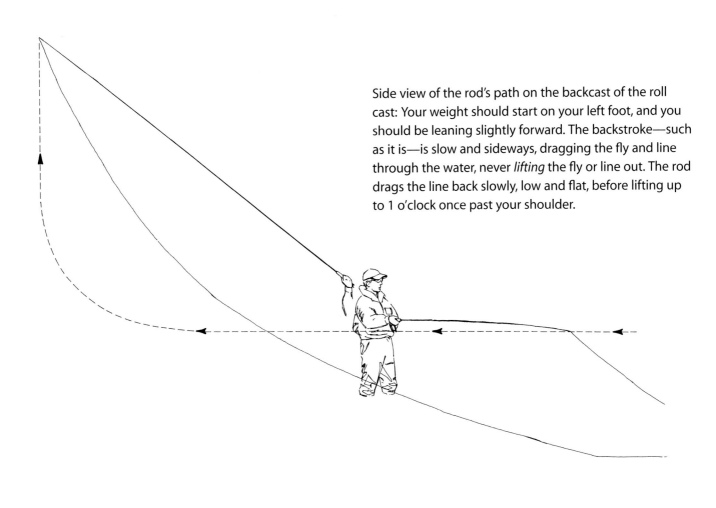

Side view of the rod's path on the backcast of the roll cast: Your weight should start on your left foot, and you should be leaning slightly forward. The backstroke—such as it is—is slow and sideways, dragging the fly and line through the water, never *lifting* the fly or line out. The rod drags the line back slowly, low and flat, before lifting up to 1 o'clock once past your shoulder.

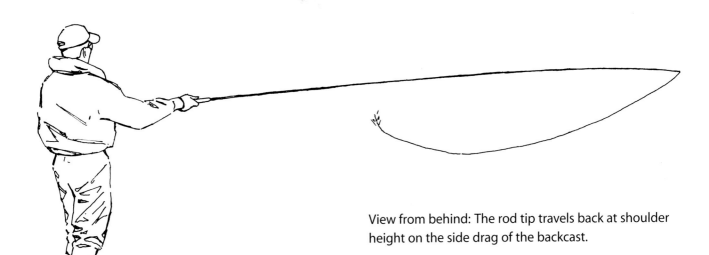

View from behind: The rod tip travels back at shoulder height on the side drag of the backcast.

Draw the rod to the side on the backcast so that the line
does not lie on the rod at the end of backcast, which can
cause tangles.

belly

point P

The forward cast should start with the rod high at
1 o'clock, the belly hanging behind the rod, and point P
in front of you. Your body weight is now mostly on your
right leg.

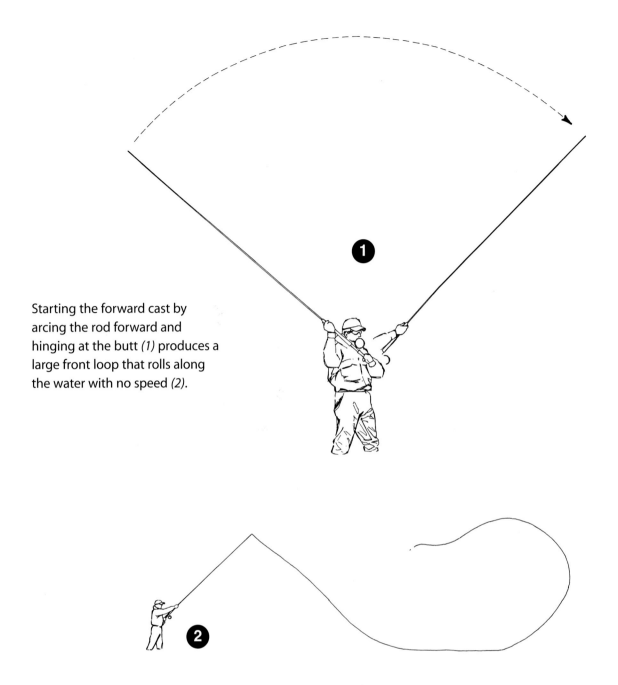

Starting the forward cast by arcing the rod forward and hinging at the butt *(1)* produces a large front loop that rolls along the water with no speed *(2)*.

The forward cast starts with leaning your body and transferring the weight back from the right foot (the rear foot) to the left foot. Toward the end of the weight transfer, both arms drive forward smoothly, though accelerating, until fully in front of you. The real trick here is to keep the rod steady at approximately a 45-degree angle through the entire arm drive. Do not arc the rod over during the forward drive. This takes all the power from the forward stroke and drives the line into a crumply heap in front of you. Once the arms have reached their extension, the power stroke begins. To gain maximum power of the forward stroke, three things happen at the same time. The bottom hand (in this case the left) sharply pulls the rod butt back toward your body. The upper hand (the right) snaps the elbow straight, and the right wrist crisply flicks forward. The bottom hand should generate about 60 percent of the power and the upper hand only 40 percent. This takes some getting used to. In most cases, casters beginning to spey cast for the first time, having had some previous single hand rod experience, use their upper hand to generate all the forward power. When they try to apply the pull of the bottom hand, all they succeed in doing is driving the rod tip down in front, instead of out in a straight line. Persistent

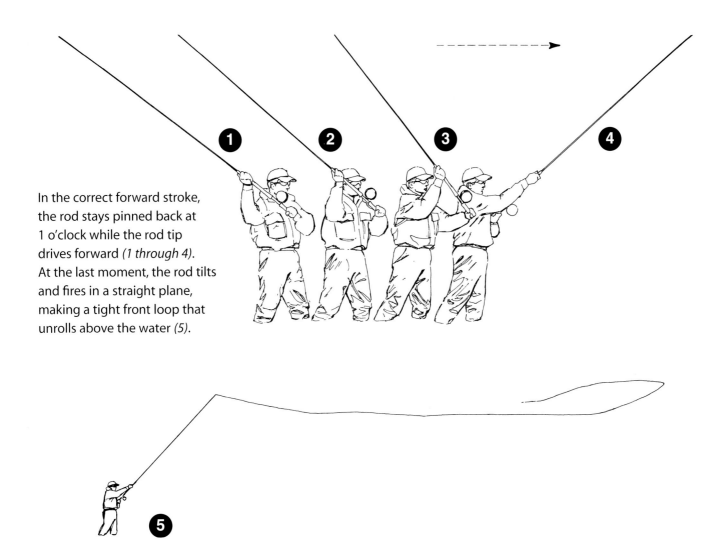

In the correct forward stroke, the rod stays pinned back at 1 o'clock while the rod tip drives forward *(1 through 4)*. At the last moment, the rod tilts and fires in a straight plane, making a tight front loop that unrolls above the water *(5)*.

practice is usually needed to get the bottom hand tugging and yet keeping the rod tip traveling horizontally. Practice, practice, practice. The rewards are really worth it.

One thing to be careful of on the forward cast is the tailing loop. This is where your forward loop unrolls from the bottom of the line instead of unrolling in a smooth parallel loop. There are a number of causes for a tailing loop. If you start the forward stroke too fast and too sharply you will get a tailing loop. You'll also have little line speed and a forward loop that climbs in the air. Another cause for a tailing loop is stopping the rod too vertically

and suddenly with a locked and wooden upper arm, instead of relaxing the grip and having a smooth steady stop with a little follow through of the rod tip. Another common cause of the tailing loop is when the belly and forward cast are not lined up in a 180-degree plane. If the belly is out of line by 15 degrees or so, you will not only get a tailing loop on the forward cast, but you will see the line collide with itself as the line tries to travel in a different direction to where you are firing the rod. I call this the collision loop.

As with all spey casts, aim the forward stroke of the roll cast as near and as parallel as possible to the line lying on the water. The wider the angle between where the line is lying on the water and where the forward cast is aimed, the worse the result will be.

To avoid tangles, wind knots, and even injury from a fly flicking up into your body, never cross the fly line lying on the water with the forward cast.

Crossing over the line on the forward cast can cause
tangles, wind knots, and frayed tempers. Look at the line
on the water and aim somewhere to the clear side.

THE 5 MOST COMMON ERRORS

1. **Problem:** A lot of stick and a lack of energy on the forward stroke.

   Cause: Coming back too fast with the rod and throwing some line, and in particular point P, behind you.

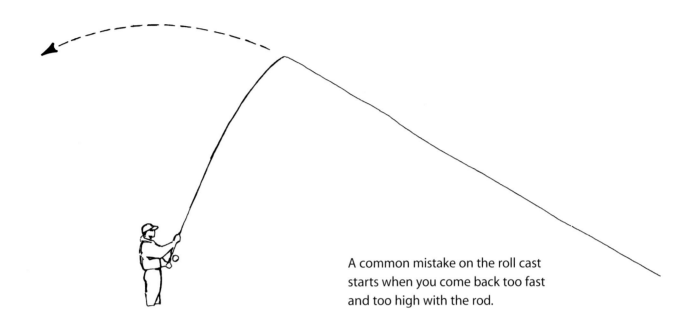

A common mistake on the roll cast starts when you come back too fast and too high with the rod.

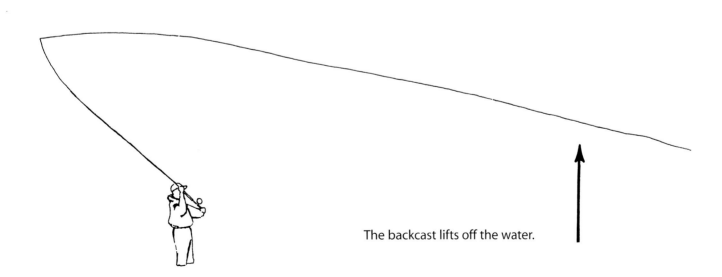

The backcast lifts off the water.

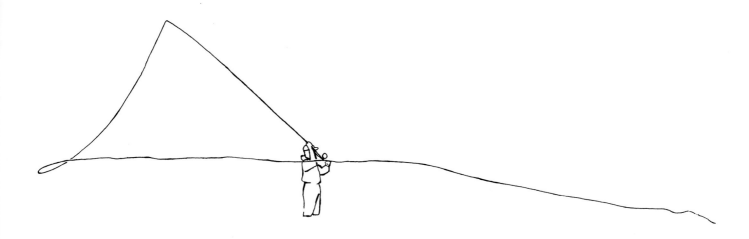

The belly goes behind you.

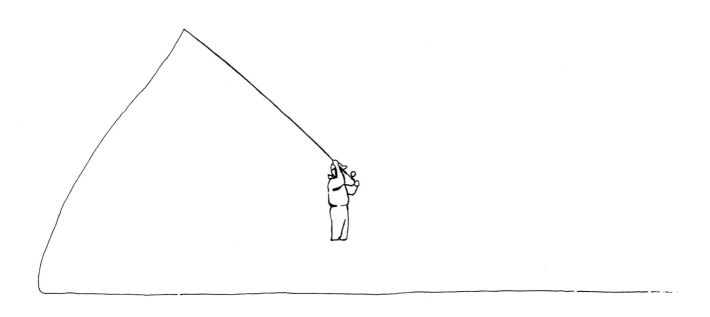

And point P lands behind you.

Hitting the forward stroke too early, instead of smoothly building up speed, results in a high climbing loop with no line speed or energy.

2. **Problem:** As the forward cast starts, there is no load and the line is tangled around the rod tip.

   Cause: Coming back too vertical with the rod and laying the fly line on top of the rod, tangling itself up.

3. **Problem:** No load on the rod as the forward cast is started.

   Cause: Not waiting for a belly to form behind the rod.

4. **Problem:** The fly line has no speed on the forward cast and unrolls with a large loop and collapses in the water, not unrolling in the air.

   Cause: Rolling the rod forward, instead of driving out in a straight line.

5. **Problem:** The forward loop attempts to unroll extremely high, with no energy, most likely creating a tailing loop.

   Cause: Starting the forward stroke with a sharp snatch, rather than a smooth push.

The roll cast is the only cast that can be successfully completed with a bunch of slack line lying in the water in front of you before you start the cast. In fact, one of the two principle uses of the roll cast is to straighten out slack line, in readiness for a different cast. The other use is to bring a deeply sunk fly, or line, up toward the surface in order to spey cast it out again. More details can be found in chapter 25.

Due to its slow, easy nature, the roll cast is certainly the best way of learning to cast with your "other" hand: the left hand for right-handed casters and the right for the left-handed. This cast is mastered by practice on still water, rather than on a faster-moving river.

One of my favorite little stories that I have heard over the years has nothing to do with fishing. A pro golfer played a wonderful round of golf and easily won the tournament he was in. A young reporter interviewing him later commented on a particular shot and told him how lucky he was to have gotten out of that difficult situation. The golfer replied, "Yeah, it's funny that. The harder I practice, the luckier I get!"

Casting is the same, though I would like to add something to the story—*good* practice is important. Take enough time to ensure that you are practicing the right things—not ingraining some fault that will be hard to get rid of later. Above all, *think* when you are practicing. Don't put your mind on autopilot and just cast. Remember the basics and make sure they are what you are practicing.

Things to think about when practicing the roll cast:

1. Start the draw back for the backcast slowly, and make sure that the rod is drawn back to your side and then slowly up to 1 o'clock behind you.

2. Hold the rod still, and wait for the belly to form behind the rod.

3. Start the forward cast slowly and smoothly and while point P is still in front.

4. Aim the forward cast directly away from the belly and as near to the line lying on the water as possible, accelerating into the power stroke.

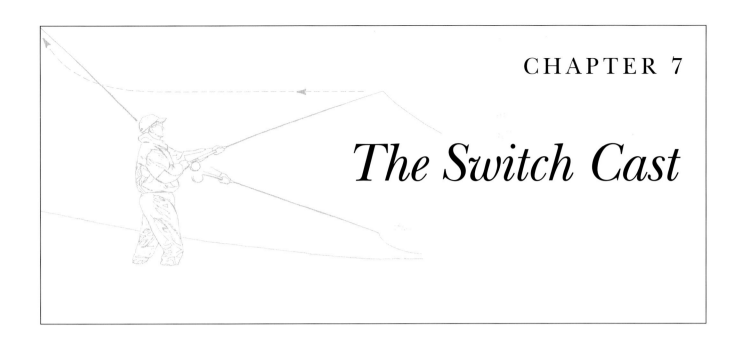

CHAPTER 7

The Switch Cast

BACKGROUND

The switch cast (also known as the forward spey, the live line roll, and the jump roll) is one of the most wonderful casts in the spey family. It is a cast of beauty, rhythm, and elegance and is perfectly suited to those that love casting for casting's sake. When you are really in the rhythm of switch casting, there is immense pleasure in getting the cast right and continuously false casting the line—not being troubled by the current swinging the fly round to the dangle (where your fly line has swung around as far as possible and is hanging straight downstream) or getting interrupted by a fish taking the fly!

This cast is not a change of direction cast, which means that you can easily practice it successfully on a lake or pond. Alternatively, on a river, the same effect can be achieved by casting your line back to the dangle repeatedly. Just make sure your line has washed completely straight before starting the next switch cast.

The switch cast is one of the greatest ways to get a strong foundation and really get into the rhythm and timing of the spey casts. In fact, in many cases, I have found that if I teach beginners the switch cast and get them to a stage where they are pretty competent with this cast, they then pick up the single spey more quickly than if they grind through the single spey on its own. The switch cast is also a cast I advocate for the occasional fisher at the start of his

Why use it? Not wanting to change direction, long line, obstacles behind.

When to use it? An excellent way of practicing the rhythm of spey casting (especially for the first half hour of fishing) and getting extra distance after a spey cast.

Which hand to use? Either.

Group? Splash and go.

annual fishing trip. Half an hour with no fly on at the beginning of the first day of the fishing trip really gets the fisher warmed up and gets the timing and muscle memory going. If you loosen up this way, the spey casts tend to come back much quicker than if you try to struggle through the week to get the casts right with the fly on and your mind dwelling on catching supper!

The switch cast has been around for a long time, though it has gone through some changes over the years. In Jock Scott's book, *Fine and Far Off*, he describes the switch casting skills of a Scotsman by the name of Alexander Grant. Jock Scott talks about the "switch of the southron—as used in tournaments. . . . The cast consists of drawing the line slowly back toward your body and then driving it away by main force." In another great old book, *Salmon Fishing* by Eric Taverner, the author says about the switch cast, "The rod is then raised to the vertical. The line will follow the point back in a deep sagging belly and the fly will remain in the water." Both these descriptions fit the *roll* cast perfectly and I would hazard a guess that the name roll cast was not known in those days. Nowadays the switch cast has evolved into a separate cast from the roll cast or, to be more accurate, into a very much improved roll cast that bears little similarity to the switch cast mentioned in these two fine books.

Both books are well worth reading for anyone interested in the history and development of spey casting. However, like many true fishermen, Jock Scott seems to have exaggerated: "Mr. Grant shot no line at all: he picked up and threw the entire 56 yards (168 feet) in one effort." Scott describes the line as a continuous taper. I have seen some of the best spey casters in the world in action, and even with the advent of ultra-powerful rods and modern spey lines (that shoot prodigious distances), very few casters can come close to shooting that amount of line, never mind picking it up and casting it without shooting! I will probably be shot and burned at the stake, but I don't see that this distance is possible now, yet alone back in the 1800s, without shooting some line.

HOW TO

As with the roll cast, it is important to start with a reasonable length of line off the reel. Forty to 45 feet of line is suitable for a 12-foot rod, 45 to 50 feet for a 13-foot rod, 50 to 55 feet for a 14-foot rod, and 55 to 60 feet for a 15-foot rod. It is very important that the line is completely straight on the water before starting this cast.

You need to remember that flat is good! The flatter the path of the rod tip, the tauter the line and the more contact you have with the load of the rod. This move should be emphasized with each spey cast and you will do well to try to keep it in mind.

There are a couple of points to get right with this move. While the rod is being swept sideways, it neither rises nor dips. The sweep should be smooth with only a slight acceleration as the rod lifts to 1 o'clock. This sweep and lift should pick the fly and line out of the water with just enough power to allow the tip of the fly line to land about 3 feet in front of your feet, but some 10 or 12 feet to the right side. Too hard a sweep and the fly rushes behind and lands in the bushes. Too slow a sweep and the fly line doesn't lift out of the water at all on the backstroke. The position of the line tip along with the timing of the forward stroke determine the success of the cast. It is better to concentrate on getting the line tip's position right on the water before ever thinking of starting the forward stroke.

Your weight should be on your left foot, and you should be leaning slightly forward (for the right hand upper-most). The rod starts low and pointing directly downstream with all the line washed tight. The cast starts with a slow and smooth lift up to about 10 o'clock.

The backcast starts with an outswinging sweep, the rod staying as far to the side as possible and traveling flat around behind you with no lift nor dip on the sweep.

The rod rises to 1 o'clock directly opposite the target at the end of the backcast. There should be enough speed in the sweep to get all the line airborne. As you can see here, the line should still be airborne when the rod gets to 1 o'clock.

Most times an anchor point that is too far behind the caster is caused by either sweeping the rod back too fast or lifting it too much.

Analogies are a great way for people to get a picture of something strange to them, and I use them a lot, particularly when I teach casting. With simple analogies, it is easier for a caster to spot a mistake and correct it when there is no instructor around. For example, where the line tip position is the key, think of a golfer on the putting green. The green is level and the ball only 3 feet from the hole. The golfer swings the putter and knocks the ball 30 feet. What went wrong? The caster who is trying to place the line tip only 3 feet from his toes on the back sweep has the same challenge. If the line tip goes 20 feet behind the caster, the backstroke is too hard. Should the line tip land 20 feet in front of the caster, then the backstroke is too soft. There is another factor that makes it difficult to place the line tip in the right place, and that is the height that the rod travels on the backstroke. If the rod travels back at the right speed but rises as it comes back instead of traveling flat, then the line tip will likely shoot behind the caster into the bushes again. Or, if the rod dips, or starts too low, the anchor point will be too far in front to get a decent belly.

An anchor point that is too far in front of the caster may result from starting the cast with slack in the line. It may also be caused by making too slow a back sweep or starting with the rod tip too high. When the line tip lands too far in front of the caster, a small belly results, which will require more power on the forward cast than the correctly positioned anchor does.

This is a great example of how low and flat the rod path should be on the backcast. For most of the sweep, the rod should travel under shoulder height.

The caster should try to land the tip of the line (the anchor point) just in front of himself and 10 feet or so to the side.

The rod has started the forward cast and is well loaded. The caster must time this so that the rod starts to move forward as soon as the line tip touches the water—splash and go. Be careful of anticipating the forward stroke with a soft forward drift, called creep. This is a common problem, resulting in only half a forward stroke and a distinct lack of line speed.

The correct path of the rod tip at the start of the backstroke (1) lifts and sweeps under the shoulder (2) with a slight acceleration as the rod curls up toward 1 o'clock (3).

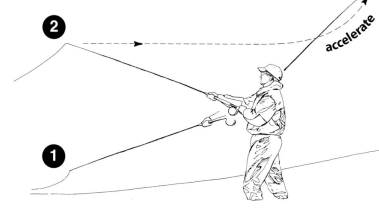

Too long a pause on the backcast and the belly falls on the water behind you—too much stick for the cast to work.

The other aspect that affects the cast, as in all the spey casts, is the line stick. For a cast to succeed, there must be a definite anchor point before starting the forward stroke, though the smaller this is the easier it is to cast. The three common causes of too much line stick are bad timing, a level drop, and the trunk.

1. **Bad Timing.** Remember the saying, "Splash and go." This is how you should respond to the back-cast. The instant the first piece of fly line touches the water (splash), you must start the forward stroke (go). If you wait a moment too long, then gravity comes into play and pulls the rest of the fly line onto the water, creating stick.

As the line comes back through the air, it should travel in a slight incline so that it is easy to time the forward cast when the first foot of line touches the water.

2. **The Level Drop.** Timing is all very well if the fly line drops to water in a slight incline. Then you can judge the forward cast when only one foot of line has touched the water. If, however, the line drops to the water in a level plane, it is either all *out* of the water or all *in* the water—no chance for success.

In this case it will be impossible to time the forward cast accurately as a lot of line will land on the water at the same instant (the level drop).

3. **The Trunk.** Without doubt the most common cause of too much line stick is the trunk. It is the hardest fault to cure on your own. Even with an instructor pointing out the problem, it is tough to overcome. It is caused by an exuberant bottom hand on the backstroke of the cast. Most casters want to put a little power into the bottom hand on the backstroke, which works very well if it is controlled, but usually ends up by throwing the rod tip down behind. The moment the rod tip starts to drop at the end of any backstroke, the line will fall into the water and stick. And this means there will be slack in the line when the forward stroke starts.

The trunk is a common cause of line stick. Point P is too far behind the caster, making too much line lie on the water. A forward cast would go nowhere because all the energy would be lost trying to break the surface tension.

Although I mention these three causes of line stick here, in the switch cast chapter, do not think that they are confined to the switch cast alone. Too much line stick will make every spey cast fail.

Now, back to where I left off. The backstroke is complete, the rod is raised to 1 o'clock and is opposite the target, and the tip of the fly line has just touched the water. You can now start the forward cast as you learned it in the chapter on roll casting. The only difference between the forward stroke of the roll cast and the switch cast is the temptation to creep forward, anticipating the forward stroke landing and losing half the forward stroke length. Keep the rod still, unless you are drifting back, until the line tip anchors; only then should any forward movement start.

THE 5 MOST COMMON ERRORS

1. **Problem:** Unable to get any control of the backstroke and the position of the anchor.

   Cause: The fly line lying on the water is too slack to start the cast.

If you start a switch cast with slack in the line, you cannot land the anchor in the right place.

2. **Problem:** Not landing the anchor point in the right position on the backstroke.

   Cause: The line is too far in front and there hasn't been enough power (or the rod started too low). The line is too far behind and the "throw" was too hard or the rod rose too steeply. The right position is between 3 feet in front and 3 feet behind your body, and 12 to 15 feet to the side.

3. **Problem:** There is a crumpled anchor where the fly line anchors on the backstroke—not a tight, straight anchor.

   Cause: The rod has dipped somewhere during the backstroke.

4. **Problem:** Too much line stick.

   Cause: Usually caused by the trunk, too long a pause, or a level drop. Listen to the sound the line makes as it leaves the water. If it slurps or makes a sound like someone drinking soup, there is too much stick.

A forward stroke with too much power too soon results in a high, climbing loop with no energy.

5. **Problem:** The forward loop unrolls too high and with little power.

   Cause: Starting the forward stroke with a sharp snatch, rather than a smooth push.

   Things to think about when practicing the switch cast:

1. Start with a tight line and the rod at about 10 o'clock.

2. Sweep the rod to the side, *flat,* and then up behind you to 1 o'clock, opposite your target.

3. Watch the line tip anchor and start the forward stroke immediately when it touches the water.

4. Drive the forward cast out as near to the line lying on the water in front of you.

CHAPTER 8

Crude, Traditional, and Modern Spey Casting

There is no single person who is credited with developing spey casting. It has evolved over the course of time because fly fishers needed to cast a fly without backcasting. Many casters claim to have developed a cast only to find there is someone else doing the same thing. Good casters adapt casts to get around a problem, and with so many good casters around, soon enough some caster somewhere will discover the very same cast you invented.

Over its history spey casting has developed different styles. As more thought has gone into the way the casts work, and new developments in the tackle industry have resulted in lighter and faster action rods, the style of the casts has changed. I have found three distinct and different spey-casting styles: the crude spey, the traditional spey, and the modern spey.

THE CRUDE SPEY

This is the earliest form of spey casting, developed over one hundred fifty years ago. Modern spey casting has evolved from this very basic technique.

Although it was very inefficient, it still has a valuable place in the modern spey caster's repertoire.

The crude spey was developed from the roll cast. Most anglers can make a roll cast, whether they have fished two-handed rods or not. The problem with the roll cast is that it is pretty useless for changing direction. You cannot cross over the line on the forward cast of the roll cast, and if you make too wide an angle change, you end up with a very poor, sloppy roll cast. So, to roll cast, the line already has to be lying in the direction you're after for any chance of success. This creates no problem when you're fishing a lake or small creek, but on a large river, when the line has swung to the dangle and is under a bank and you want to cast back across the river, you cannot do that by roll casting. To get around this, the early spey casters used to dump the line across the river with a very vigorous backhand stroke. As the line lands on the water in a dribbly puddle, the rod is drawn back and the roll cast is used to finish off the cast with a nicely presented fly. The first spey cast was born. I call it the crude spey and here's how to do it:

Standing very close to obstructions can be a problem
even for a spey cast. Start with the line out and washed
tight downstream.

Swing the rod in toward the near bank and lift to about 11 o'clock.

Accelerate the rod tip in an up-and-over type of movement toward the center of the river, throwing the line across toward the far bank. The line lands in a heap in front of you, slightly upstream of where you are standing.

Don't worry if the anchor lands in a bit of a heap; that's just the way this cast works.

Before the current washes the line back downstream, draw the rod around on the upstream shoulder and behind you to form a small belly, holding the rod high and keeping the line away from the bushes.

Punch the forward cast out hard and as near as you can
to the anchor without crossing the line. Drive the rod tip
straight out to get a reasonable forward loop.

The crude spey is simple, requires no real skill, and works fairly well, though these days very few casters use it, as it is too inefficient.

A few years ago I was fishing the Long Pool on the Rothes beat of the river Spey. The river was high and impossible to wade, and to fish the pool successfully I had to hop from one big rock to the next, standing about 3 feet above the water. I found it very hard to use a modern spey cast, as the moment I completed any form of backstroke, my line would catch one of the rocks or the weeds growing out of the rocks behind me. After a frustrating ten minutes, I hit on the idea of using the crude spey. The advantage of the crude spey is that the cast is broken into two separate movements—the flop across the water, and then the draw back and roll forward. The pause between the flop and the draw back means that there is no momentum back into the bank behind you and, therefore, absolutely no kind of backcast. The cast worked like a dream and I managed to fish the whole pool out without catching another rock or weed! Of course, it is not really an efficient cast, so the distance I was fishing was less than normal. But at least I managed to fish a pool that otherwise would have caused a headache.

The problem with the modern and traditional speys is that they need some space behind—even if it is only 1 foot. The crude spey needs zero! Since that experience on the Spey, I have taught this cast in my schools and, I hope, prepared casters for any nasty situations they are likely to come across.

THE TRADITIONAL SPEY
The crude spey was soon refined to the traditional spey. There seemed little point in stopping the cast between the flop across the river and the roll cast. So, while the rod tip follows the same path as the crude spey, it does not stop after the flop across but immediately pulls round to the upstream shoulder and up to 1 o'clock *before* any part of the line touches the water. Once the fly line has landed, you start the forward cast and drive the line out in front. Not only does the continuous speed of the backcast result in more energy in the line (and thus a farther cast), but the cast now looks very pretty and flowing.

For many years, this was spey casting. Traditional spey casting worked very well with softer action rods and was (and is) instantly recognizable by the loops and figure-eight movements that the rod tip takes.

While a lot more efficient than the crude spey, the traditional style is still limited in the distance it casts, compared to the modern style. The problem with the traditional style is that the big figure eights and loops of the rod tip do little to improve the distance the line will travel. The most useless direction that a rod can travel when you're spey casting is vertically down. A downward moving rod tip cannot move the line forward, or backward, an inch. The only direction that really effects how far a line will travel is horizontal. This is the downside of the traditional style. All the loops and moves look wonderful but are very inefficient with regard to getting maximum distance and expending minimum effort.

THE MODERN SPEY
The modern spey, or more accurately the modern spey style, relies on much flatter movements of the rod tip. This is only possible with faster-action rods, as the soft, traditional-action rods flex too much to keep the rod tip traveling in a straight line.

Not only do the flatter movements mean the caster uses less energy to complete the cast, but all the speed generated from the rod tip is transmitted to the fly line, directly. Whereas with any down movement of the rod, some of the energy used to move the rod is lost.

Being a fan and practitioner of the modern style, I shall be describing techniques in the next few chapters that are based on these flatter, energy efficient, and dynamic movements.

The modern style of spey casting uses much flatter rod
movements and faster rod actions than the traditional
style.

The rod lifts no higher than this throughout the backcast, and stays flat until the slight raise at the very end of the stroke. Perfect modern spey style.

The rod is still low and flat as it reaches behind the caster.
This more advanced technique is covered in more detail
in chapter 14.

CHAPTER 9

The Single Spey

BACKGROUND

The single spey is the most useful of all the spey casts. It is also the most efficient and will cast the line farther than any other spey cast. The cast works best through a fine change of angle 25 to 40 degrees, although it is possible to change the line direction up to 180 degrees. Since there are three distinct forms of the single spey and all will work and serve their purpose, it is really up to you to find the style of cast that suits you.

The delivery of this cast is always made from the upstream shoulder, regardless of which side of the river you are on, and that is why practice with both hands is essential. If you are standing on the left bank (river flowing from right to left), looking across the river, the right hand is on the upstream side. Therefore "right hand up" is used on the left bank. Conversely, on the right bank the left hand is used (for backhanded, with the right hand off the left shoulder), as this is the upstream arm. This is the nature of the beast. I have seen some casters do a type of inside spey, where the basic single spey is used with the downstream arm, but I find this inefficient and ineffective for achieving line speed and distance.

HOW TO

I generally teach beginners what I call the alpine spey. Most novice spey casters don't have the ability to get a good single spey with the flatter movements that are so effective, so I start them off with this

Why use it? To change direction, with a long line, obstacles behind.
When to use it? Upstream wind.
Which hand to use? Left hand up on the right bank of the river. Right hand up on the left bank.
Group? Splash and go.

alpine spey. Anyone who has spent any time spey casting will have heard that the single spey is the most difficult spey cast to master, although with a clear picture in your mind, it can be a lot easier to learn than you think.

The alpine spey is so named because I use the analogy of two sharp, pointed mountains to get you to draw the correct rod path. The first mountain peak is about 45 degrees across the river on the opposite bank, and the second mountain peak is directly behind you and exactly opposite where the forward cast is going to go. Connecting these two mountains is a long sweeping valley. Using the alpine spey concept, you start the rod tip pointing at the base of the first mountain on the left hand slope. The rod travels up the left slope of the mountain to the summit (vertically—a cliff face) then rapidly travels down the right-hand slope, along the flat valley, and up to the top of the second mountain behind you. There is a brief pause for the line to touch the water (splash and go), and then the rod tip jumps across from the top of the second mountain to the top of the first.

It is tough to get a clear picture of the cast from these few words, so the photos give you a better idea of the shape the rod tip should travel. What the words can do is give you an idea of the speed the rod tip should travel. Imagine your rod tip is following a climber on the two mountains. He is going to climb the mountain slowly. When he gets to the summit, he will ski down rapidly, much faster than he climbs, and the momentum of his skis takes him all the way to the top of the second mountain. At the top of that mountain, he pauses and then jumps to try to reach the summit of the first mountain. The rod travels at the same speeds as the skier—in other words, start the initial lift slowly, accelerate into the downward dip, keep the speed up through the dip and the lift to 1 o'clock, pause, and then accelerate through the forward stroke.

Here is the cast in caster's lingo, not in mountaineer's! (In the following series of photographs, I have wrapped the line around the rod to give a clear indication of the path the rod takes.)

The line has swung around in the river to the dangle, and you want to cast your fly back across the river at an angle of 60 degrees or so. Stand with your left foot forward (weight mostly on this foot) and angled toward the target. In your mind, draw an imaginary line on the water, directly between your foot and the target. I call this the orange line. Point the rod slightly out across the river, but keep it low and make sure the line is still tight on the dangle.

Begin the cast by lifting the rod smoothly and vertically in front of you to about 11 o'clock—being careful not to move the rod to either side as you lift.

point P

A high lift and early start of the backstroke ensures that point P runs all the way to the line tip, as far from you as possible. This results in a clean backstroke, easily breaking the water tension.

point P

A pause at the top of the lift lets the line and point P sag back toward you, resulting in too much line on the water and making it difficult to position the anchor.

As soon as the rod has reached the summit of the lift, start to dip it with a slight acceleration.

Continue the back sweep, keeping the rod flat and accelerating slightly.

Finish with the rod raised toward 1 o'clock and directly opposite the target off your right shoulder. This dip is best achieved by transferring your body weight from your front foot to your back foot and rotating your hips. This dip should resemble a smile or a curtsy or a saucer or any other similarly shaped object you can think of. The angle of descent of the dip should be relatively gentle and the depth no more than 4 to 5 feet. Wait in the 1 o'clock position until the first piece of fly line (the anchor point) touches the water.

The forward cast is just starting (you can see the rod flexed slightly) as the line tip touches the water—splash and go.

This is about getting the setup right (and, of course, the timing). Practice is again the key to success. Don't worry too much at the start with the way the cast goes out on the forward stroke. The best practice is with the backstroke, to make sure that the setup is right and the *potential* of the cast is there. Like all spey casts, the first thing to master is the shape, or path, that the rod tip travels. Once that is correct, start to concentrate on the speed the rod moves to position the anchor point correctly, and

finally, worry about getting your timing right. Without the rod traveling in the right path, you may as well roll the line into a ball and throw it into the river for all the effect it will have.

The wider the angle change you want to make with the single spey, the bigger the lift at the beginning of the cast and the deeper the dip needs to be. More speed is needed in the dip and more rotation in the body to get the rod and D loop opposite the target.

THE 5 MOST COMMON ERRORS

The four illustrations depict the path the rod tip should travel, viewed from the caster's eyes. To get an accurate picture of how the rod should travel, look at these four illustrations by holding the book vertically and follow the lines with your index finger, starting at X. The movement your finger makes corresponds to that of the rod. There should be rotation in the rod (and finger) so Y is directly opposite your target. You may need to bend the page to see this.

1. **Problem:** Getting the line caught around the body as the backcast starts.

   Cause: Most casters attempting the lift at the start of the cast have a drift lift. As the rod lifts at the beginning of the cast, it tends to drift sideways in anticipation of the dip. This can really effect where the anchor point lands, although it is not impossible to get right. It is also very likely to lead to too much line stick on the water, as well as a bloody L. Do make sure that the initial lift is slow and *vertical*. Wrapping the line around your body can also be caused by pointing too much across the river at the start of the cast and having slack in the line before the cast starts.

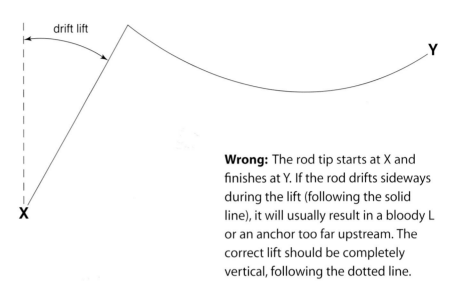

Wrong: The rod tip starts at X and finishes at Y. If the rod drifts sideways during the lift (following the solid line), it will usually result in a bloody L or an anchor too far upstream. The correct lift should be completely vertical, following the dotted line.

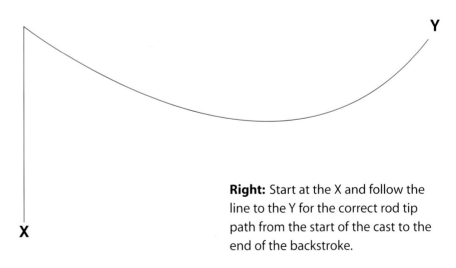

Right: Start at the X and follow the line to the Y for the correct rod tip path from the start of the cast to the end of the backstroke.

2. **Problem**: Sending the anchor point too far upstream and getting a bloody L.

Cause: Many casters do a thing I call Aussie style. At the top of the lift (at the beginning of the cast), the rod should dip instantly. Aussie style is where the rod sweeps horizontally before the dip—even a 6-inch sideways movement before the dip will create a big problem. Most times the rod travels sideways before the dip starts it will create a bloody L and send the anchor too far upstream.

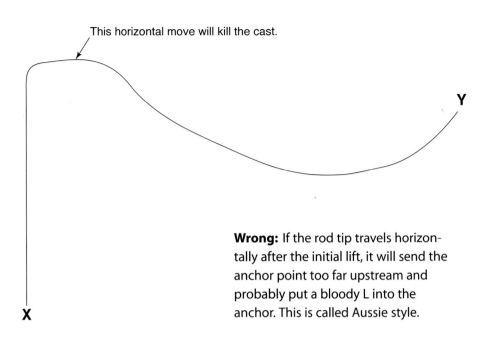

This horizontal move will kill the cast.

X **Y**

Wrong: If the rod tip travels horizontally after the initial lift, it will send the anchor point too far upstream and probably put a bloody L into the anchor. This is called Aussie style.

3. **Problem:** Not getting the anchor to land in the right place.

Cause: There are many causes of this, not the least being the first two problems above. The other common mistake that causes this is that the rod dips too steeply or not at all. Too steeply and either the anchor point lands *downstream* of your orange line or you will get a bloody L. Too shallow and the anchor point will fly past you and land way upstream of your orange line and not at all parallel to it. If the backstroke is correct, the fly line should land on the water tight, just on the upstream side of your orange line and parallel to it. Do this and the cast is set up for the perfect forward stroke.

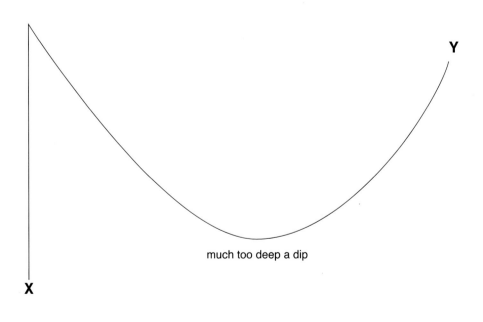

much too deep a dip

X **Y**

Wrong: Dipping too steeply and deeply will always result in a bloody L.

Too slow or too steep a dip on the backstroke results in the anchor landing too far downstream and a reverse bloody L.

Too flat or too fast a dip on the backstroke results in the anchor landing too far upstream and not fully aligned with your target. This can be caused by casting Aussie style.

4. **Problem:** There is no load on the rod as it drives out on the forward cast.

   Cause: The 180-degree principle has been broken. Either the rod or belly haven't pulled around far enough to load the rod and be opposite the intended forward stroke or target. Remember, your body should be turning from the ankles and hips.

5. **Problem:** Too much line stick.

Cause: Again, a number of likely candidates, timing (waiting too long) is one of the more common mistakes. The other is the trunk. Make sure that the rod is up toward 1 o'clock when it's behind you and that the bottom hand is close to your chest. "Left hand to your heart, laddies!"

The trunk is particularly common with the single spey and hard for the caster to spot. If you hear a slurping sound on the forward cast, the trunk was probably the culprit.

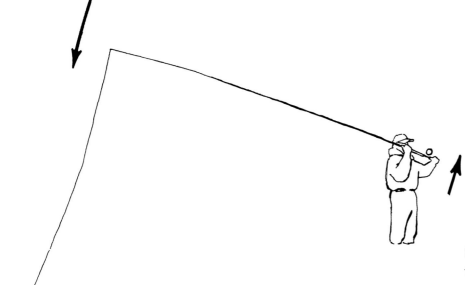

From the side you can see that the trunk causes too much line stick.

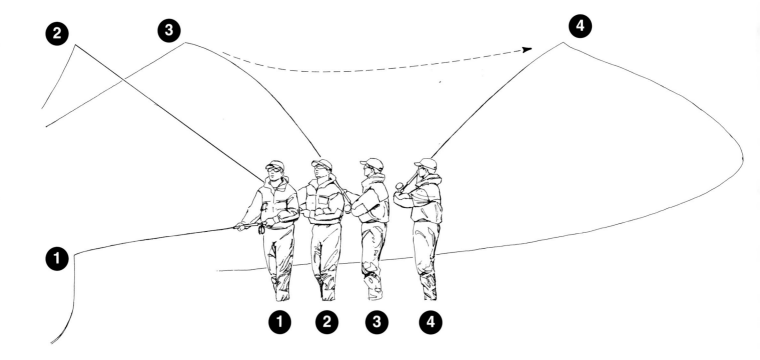

For the backstroke, point the rod slightly out toward the target *(1)*. Lift the rod to about 10 o'clock *(2)*. Start to load the rod with a shallow dip, tightening the rod against the line *(3)*. Raise the rod at the end of the dip to 1 o'clock and opposite the target *(4)*. The body turns as the backcast is made.

Things to think about when practicing the single spey cast:

1. Start with a tight line, washed downstream, and the rod low, about halfway toward your target.

2. Point. Lift. Dip. Finish with the rod tip behind you at 1 o'clock—opposite your target.

3. Watch the line tip anchor and start the forward stroke immediately when the line tip touches the water.

4. Drive the forward cast out as near to the line lying on the water in front of you as you can get it.

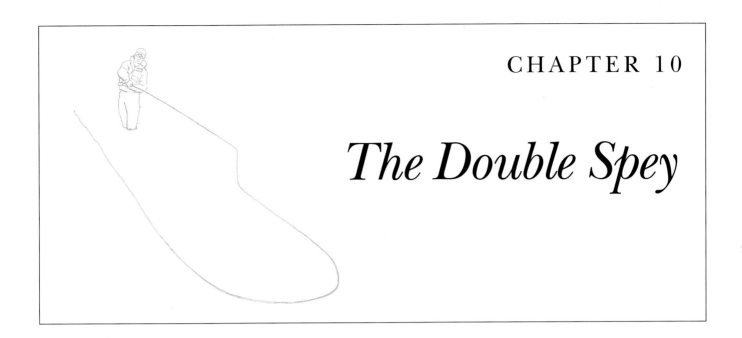

The Double Spey

BACKGROUND

The double spey is usually considered the easiest of the spey casts to learn (until the snap T was developed). It has a rhythm that is fairly easy to pick up; in fact, a lot of casters like to call it a waltz, and that reference certainly sums up the speed of each casual stroke . . . 1, 2, 3; 1, 2, 3; 1, 2, 3. It is also more difficult to make a mistake than the single spey. With the single spey, the anchor point has to be in a particular spot at the end of the backstroke, which is what makes it such a hard cast to master. With the double spey, you have much more tolerance as to where the line can land and the results (if wrong) are not so drastic.

As in all the casts, there are many variations, and few casters you watch will have the same style. The biggest difference is, once again, in the traditional style versus the modern style. The traditional double spey is a real thing of beauty. I can sit and watch a traditional double spey caster for hours, marveling at the wondrous figure-eight rod movements and the caster's control of the line. Watching the final power stroke on the forward cast with the line unrolling beautifully across the river is truly poetry in motion. I don't think the modern style is as attractive to watch, but it is much more efficient and will outcast the traditional style (with a faster rod action) by yards.

Why use it? To change direction with long line, obstacles behind.
When to use it? Downstream wind.
Which hand to use? Left hand up on the left bank of the river. Right hand up on the right bank. This maxim may help you: Remember the letter **D**. **D**o the **D**ouble spey with a **D**ownstream wind and use your **D**ownstream arm.
Group? Waterborne anchor.

One thing that confuses a lot of people is when to use which cast and with which hand. This is usually decided for you by the direction of the wind. Safety should always come first when casting, and nothing is more dangerous than casting with your right hand up when the wind is blowing onto your right hand side. The two-handed rods allow you to easily change hands and, when the wind is on the right, have the left hand up. The nature of the casts means that the double spey is always cast off the downstream shoulder, making it the safest cast when the wind is blowing onto your upstream arm. All very confusing, but with the double spey, this can be easier to remember than with the other casts, especially if you have learned the little maxim: *Do the Double spey when there is a Downstream wind and use the Downstream arm.*

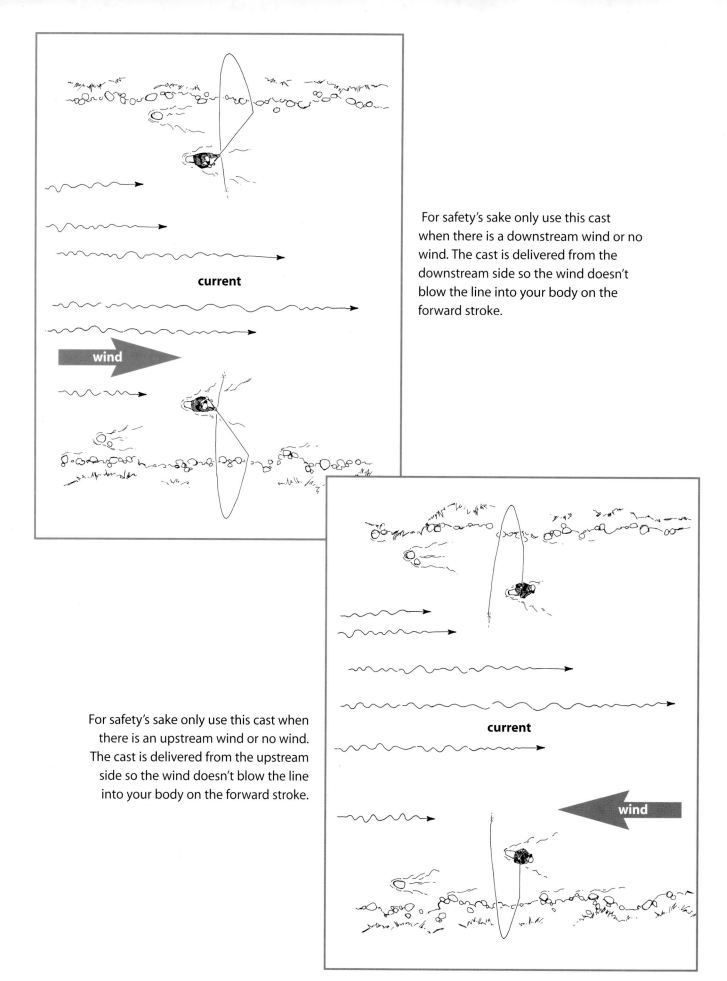

For safety's sake only use this cast when there is a downstream wind or no wind. The cast is delivered from the downstream side so the wind doesn't blow the line into your body on the forward stroke.

current

wind

For safety's sake only use this cast when there is an upstream wind or no wind. The cast is delivered from the upstream side so the wind doesn't blow the line into your body on the forward stroke.

current

wind

Start with the rod pointing downstream and 45 to 55 feet of line washed tight directly downstream of you. Make sure the line is tight and on the dangle before you start the cast. Raise the rod slowly and steadily and stop at 10 o'clock, still pointing directly downstream.

HOW TO

Assume you are going to use the right hand (right bank of the river). The line is on the dangle, and you want to cast your fly back across the river at an angle of 60 degrees or so. Stand with your left foot forward (weight mostly on this foot), angled toward the target. In your mind, draw an imaginary orange line on the water, directly between your front foot and your target.

Stage 1

Start with the rod pointing downstream and the line washed tight, directly downstream of you. Raise the rod slowly and steadily to 10 o'clock, still pointing directly downstream, and stop, waiting for the fly line you have lifted to sag to a motionless stop. Swing the rod tip over and across your body and finish pointing it directly upstream, but low to the water. The idea is to bring the tip of the fly line out

point P

Before you start stage 1, make sure the line has sagged back to the water after the initial lift and point P is close to you.

of the water on your downstream side and settle it about a rod length *downstream* of where you are standing. Too fast a movement and the fly line will pass you and land on the upstream side of your orange line. This is dangerous and you can easily hook yourself in your arm, under your chin, or wrap the hook around the rod. If the line passes you on stage 1, abort the cast, flick it back downstream, and start again. If the line lands too far downstream, there will be too much side pull to get an effective belly to load the rod. As you gain more control in the positioning of the first stage, try to land the tip (still a rod length off your downstream leg!) close to your body.

I teach my novice students to tap the water with the rod tip about 15 degrees out from the dangle,

Point P isn't even in the picture. If you start stage 1 while point P is too far downstream, the line will come out of the water too easily and fly upstream of your orange line.

making a splash with the rod tip. This splash serves as a focal point and an aim for landing the nail knot on. The cast will still work very well if the nail knot lands 8 feet above or below the splash, but it serves as a target for landing the nail knot at the end of stage 1.

A fairly simple analogy of the path the rod should take is to imagine you are standing in the middle of a room looking at a wall in front of you. Start with the rod tip pointing at the top right-hand corner of the wall in front (for the right-handed cast). Swing the rod tip along the top of the wall in front and then down to the floor in the left-hand corner. This is the basic shape, though as you perfect it you will want to round off the corner.

Sweep the rod over your head and upstream with just enough speed to lift the fly line about a foot above the water.

line tip

At the end of stage 1, the rod tip should point directly upstream, low, and flat. The nail knot at the end of the fly line should land about a rod length downstream of you and in your wading wake.

Finish stage 1 with the rod tip very low to the water,
pointing upstream and slightly in toward your bank.
Note the loop of line that is thrown upstream.

The tip of the fly line has landed upstream of the caster at the end of stage 1. If you continue with this cast, you will likely impale yourself with the hook.

This line tip has landed too far downstream at the end of
stage 1 to get enough belly to load the rod.

With the anchor landing too far downstream, a bloody L and a weak forward cast will result. As you get more controlled in the positioning of the first stage, try to land the line tip (still a rod length off your downstream leg!) close to your body.

land line tip here

Before you start, it can help to tap the water with the rod tip slightly downstream and in front of you. This serves as an aiming point for the tip of the line at the end of stage 1. The cast will still work very well if the nail knot lands 8 feet above the splash or 8 feet below it, but the splash serves as a target for landing the nail knot at the end of stage 1.

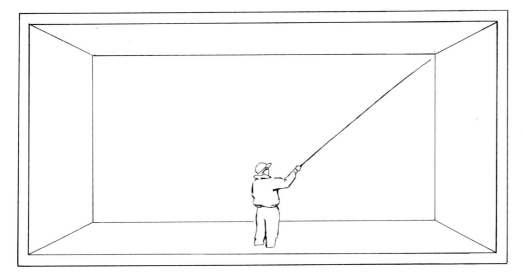

Here's the path the rod tip should take on stage 1 of the double spey (for the right-handed cast): Imagine you are standing in a room facing the front wall. Start the cast with the rod tip up in the top right-hand corner where the front wall meets the ceiling.

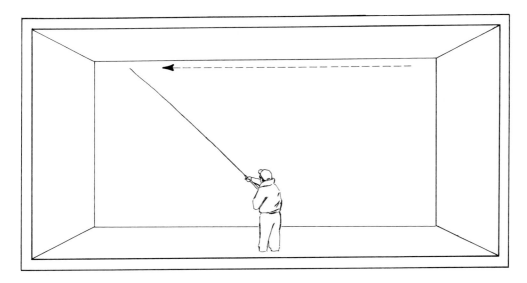

Sweep the rod along the edge of the ceiling to the upper left-hand corner.

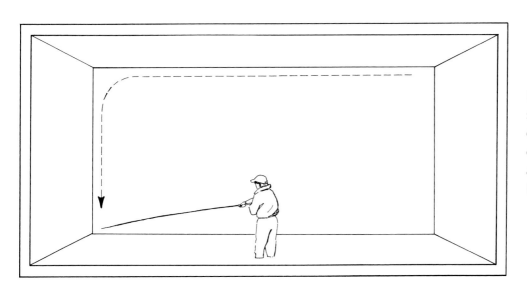

In one continuous smooth sweep, drop the rod tip down toward the corner of the floor and front wall and slightly along the left-hand wall.

white mouse
starting

Once your line has landed at the end of stage 1 and your rod tip is low, start stage 2 by smoothly sweeping the rod downstream horizontally, tearing most of the line out of the water (creating a white mouse of spray).

Stage 2

Those who know something about spey casting will note that I have a very different style compared with the traditional double spey, with its big figure-eight movements of the rod tip. These movements, particularly the downward rod movements, only serve to increase line stick and form bloody Ls. Remember, flat is good. Beware of any slight dip in the rod tip as you sweep round on stage 2. It is easy to do and very hard to spot and can drive you mad trying to figure out what is going wrong! The dip, or dreaded dip as I call it, is a cause of frustration as it results in the fly line hitting your body or your rod as you finish the sweep through on stage 2. It will also create a bloody L.

perfect white mouse

The rod tip must *never* dip on stage 2—when it reaches your downstream hip, start raising it with enough speed to keep a good white mouse.

Stage 2 finishes with the rod tip behind you at 1 o'clock and the belly opposite the target. The white mouse has run right to the end of the line tip. The idea behind this movement is to change the fly line's position from one lying on the water across your body to a mostly aerialized belly with a small anchor, pointing toward the target.

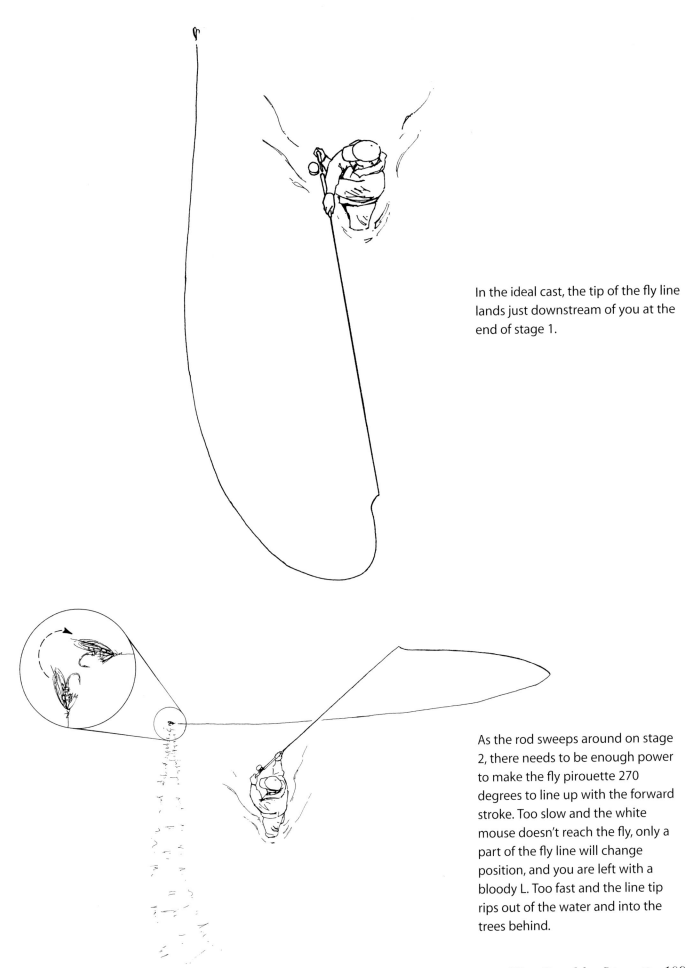

In the ideal cast, the tip of the fly line lands just downstream of you at the end of stage 1.

As the rod sweeps around on stage 2, there needs to be enough power to make the fly pirouette 270 degrees to line up with the forward stroke. Too slow and the white mouse doesn't reach the fly, only a part of the fly line will change position, and you are left with a bloody L. Too fast and the line tip rips out of the water and into the trees behind.

The bloody L is caused by sweeping stage 2 too slow or dipping in the middle of stage 2. With a short line the cast will succeed, but for distance and, of course, perfection, the bloody L slows down the forward cast and should be avoided.

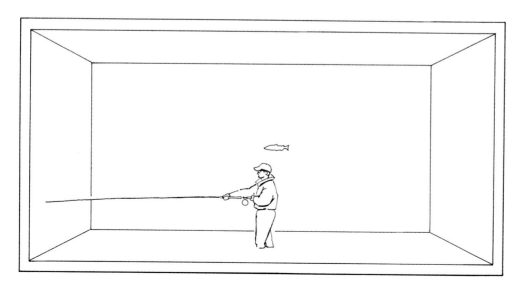

To continue with our room analogy, begin stage 2 with the rod low and flat along the left-hand wall.

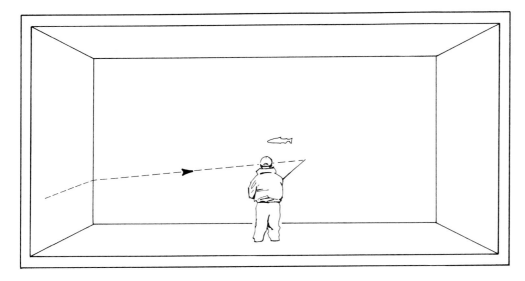

Make sure the rod stays low, traveling along the front wall with a very slight incline.

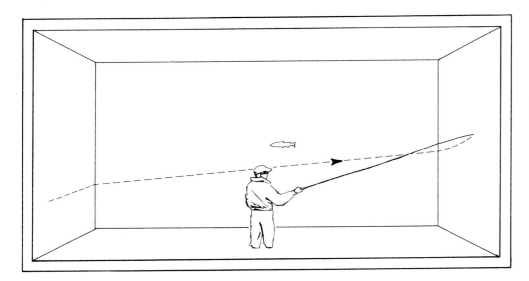

Still rising slightly, it reaches the right-hand wall.

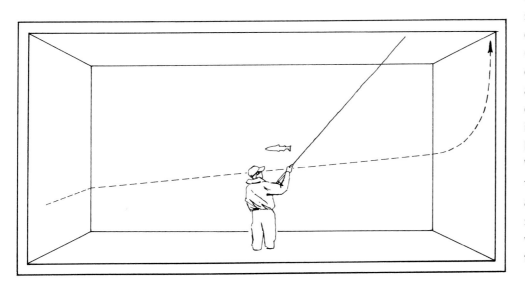

As you pass your shoulder, bring the rod tip up smoothly toward the ceiling of the right-hand wall (about 1 o'clock) directly opposite your target. Once again, the change of direction of rod, from slight incline to slight lift, should be smooth and rounded. While your rod and arms are traveling through stage 2 and up to 1 o'clock, you should transfer your body weight from your front (left) foot to your back foot.

The forward casts starts (stage 3). The belly is exactly opposite the target, and the line stick is parallel to the target.

Stage 3

Once you have finished stage 2 and formed the belly behind the rod, it is a simple matter of finishing off with the forward stroke. On this note, however, remember that timing is important and the timing between the end of stage 2 and the start of the forward stroke depends on the size and speed of the belly. The bigger the belly, the more time you have to wait for the belly to achieve its maximum size. A small belly of only 2 to 3 feet in size (necessary when you are tight to an obstruction) forms rapidly, so the forward stroke can almost be instantaneous. Some people find it easier to get the timing right by watching the belly form behind them. As the belly stops moving backwards, start the forward stroke.

Loop outbound.

Start stage 1 too low and the line tip will fly upstream past you. Before you start the double spey, lift the rod to about 10 o'clock.

THE 5 MOST COMMON ERRORS

1. **Problem:** The fly line travels too far upstream on stage 1.

   Cause: Starting the rod too low at the very beginning of stage 1. This results in too much power as you move the rod across your body and the fly and line land upstream of the orange line.

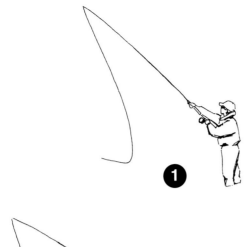

2. **Problem:** The fly line lands too far away from your body, across the river

Cause: Throwing stage 1 in an outward curve and laying the anchor point too far from your body. Ideally the fly line should end up within 5 feet of where you are standing and the nail knot about a rod length downstream of you. Bring the rod more over the top of your head on stage 1 to get the line closer.

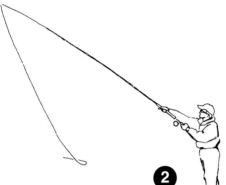

If the rod tip sweeps too far out across the river on stage 1, the fly line will lay too far from your body to get a big belly.

Here the fly line lands too far away from the caster's body because he swept the rod out across the river on stage 1. The result is a small belly, which can be useful at times when obstructions are close behind you.

This is how close to your body the fly line should land at the end of stage 1 in order to get the largest belly—not wise, though, when you are tight to bushes behind.

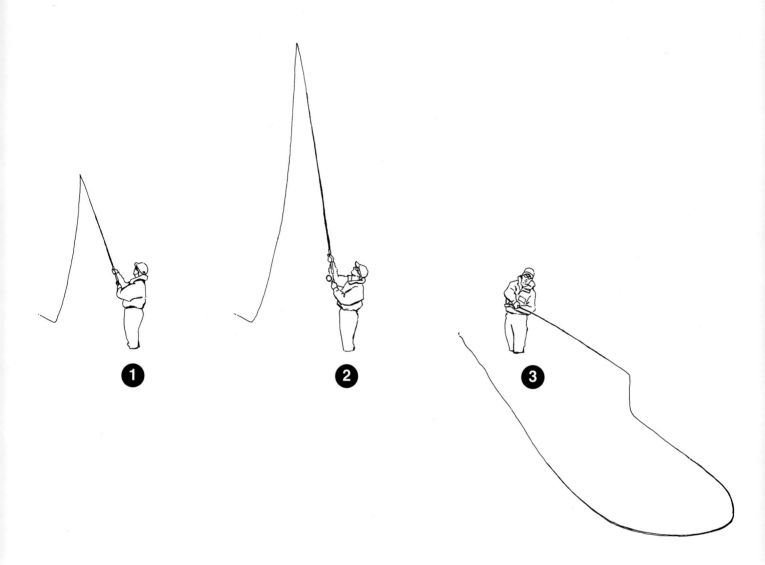

Bring the rod tip more over your head to lay the fly line within a few feet of your wading position, but keep the tip of the line slightly downstream.

Finishing stage 1 too high almost always results in the dreaded dip in stage 2 and a bloody L.

3. **Problem:** The bloody L and the line coming very close to your body as you start the forward cast.

Cause: Finishing stage 1 with the rod raised too high. This is the most common error, though only really a problem if stage 2 dips. It is much easier to dip the rod in stage 2 if the rod starts high. Start the rod tip low, and it cannot really dip!

4. **Problem:** Not getting the fly line to pirouette on the nail knot.

Cause: Misjudging the speed and height of stage 2. Remember you are trying to get the very tip of the fly line to pirouette (or slither slightly). Too fast or too high with the rod and you will end up in the bushes. Too slow or too low (or with a dip) and you will end up with the bloody L.

Hooking the rod tip too far round the back of your head is a common problem. This pulls the belly behind you and results in the belly hitting you on the forward stroke. The correct cast is shown in *1*, the incorrect one in *2*.

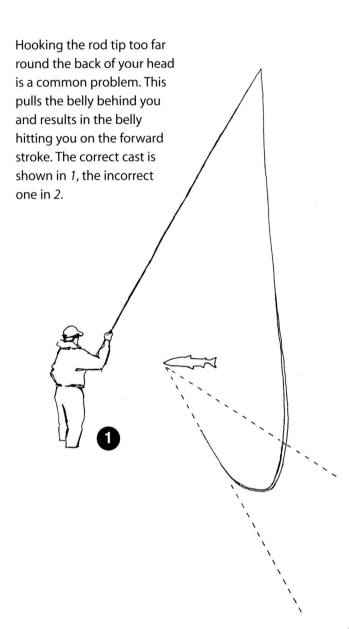

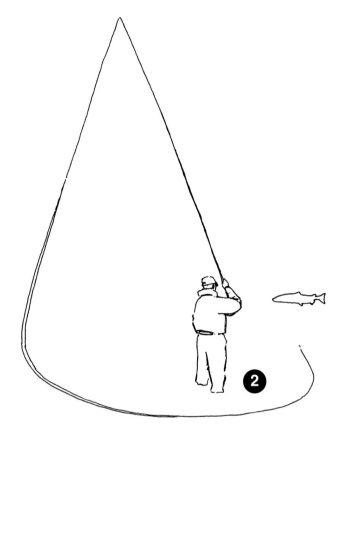

5. **Problem:** No load on the rod as the forward cast starts and the line hitting, or coming close to hitting, your body.

Cause: Hooking the belly round the back of the head too much. This occurs frequently. The third principle of spey casting is that the belly and forward stroke should line up in a 180-degree plane—ready to fire straight. The centrifugal force of stage 2 often means that the belly continues to move after the rod stops and ends up off course.

Things to think about when practicing the double spey cast:

1. Start with 45 to 55 feet of line washed tight downstream and the rod raised to about 10 o'clock.

2. Sweep the rod slightly over your head and down to the water, pointing directly upstream.

3. Bring the rod back downstream, around behind you, and up to 1 o'clock—opposite your target.

4. Wait for the fly line tip to pirouette.

5. Drive the forward cast out near to the line lying on the water in front of you.

CHAPTER 11

The Snake Roll

BACKGROUND

Many years ago my father and I ran a fly-fishing school in Devon, England, on the river Torridge. The pool we used to teach spey casting on was almost ideal. It was wide enough to throw a full line, shallow and gentle enough to wade to the other side and teach casting from both banks, and had a nice high bank from which we used to film casters. The only thing that was wrong with it was that there was not a lot of current. The caster would stand on the left bank (river flowing from right to left) cast a single spey across the pool and then have to wait quite some time for the current to wash the line back to the dangle. This got frustrating. There were too many trees lining the pool to do an overhead cast, so we used two roll casts to get the line back downstream. The first roll cast was to get the line in the right area and the second to straighten it out. Over the course of time I started to speed the two roll casts up, merging them into one fluid movement, and thus was born the snake roll. My father saw me doing this cast and recognized it as a cast in its own right with a number of fishing applications, and so we came to name it. Being a young kid in those days, I wanted to call it the sausage roll, but my father's wisdom prevailed and we called it the snake roll.

Since we started teaching this cast in the early '80s, I have seen the same cast done by many good casters and frequently heard it called by other names. This just goes to show that there is nothing

Why use it? Obstructions behind you and on the upstream shoulder, or quiet water not to be disturbed. To change direction.
When to use it? Downstream wind.
Which hand to use? Left hand up on the left bank of the river. Right hand up on the right bank.
Group? Splash and go.

new in the casting world. When you believe you have created a brand new cast, someone else has probably been doing it for years!

The snake roll as a fishing cast is used in exactly the same situation as the double spey—with a downstream wind, right hand up on the right bank, and left hand up on the left bank. So, if it is used in the same situation as the double spey, why learn it? In truth you don't need to know the snake roll or the snap T (covered in the next chapter) if you are competent with the single spey and the double spey. However, casting is a skill, and, like any other skill, we take immense satisfaction in doing something to the best of our ability, learning new skills, and being able to do everything possible. In truth, the snake roll changes direction faster than the double spey, which equates to more time with your fly in the water and, therefore, more fish. The snake roll takes about $4/7$ of the time of a double spey. In other words, in the time it takes you to do forty double speys, you could do seventy snake rolls (if you were only casting, not fishing). It also makes a lot less disturbance on the water than the double spey, and finally, some casters find it easier to learn than the double spey.

HOW TO

With the right hand up, stand on the right bank. The line is on the dangle and you want to cast your fly back across the river at an angle of 90 degrees or so. Stand with your left foot forward (weight mostly on this foot), angled toward the target, and your body facing mostly downstream. In your mind, draw the imaginary orange line on the water, directly between your front foot and your target. With the snake roll, you will draw a lower case e (counterclockwise) with the rod tip—big and bold, but finish the e by lifting the rod tip up to 1 o'clock. (In this series of photos I have wrapped the line around the rod so you can easily see the rod path without getting distracted by the line.)

What should happen, if you get the e shape right, is that the fly line will jump out of the water on the dangle and land about 10 feet to your right-hand side—dead straight and pointing toward the target.

The iron bridge pool on the river Torridge in England was the birthplace of the snake roll and the site of many spey-casting lessons.

Start the snake roll with the rod pointing downstream and level with your head.

Slowly draw the rod back behind you, keeping the rod tip
traveling flat for the first part of the **e** shape.

Smoothly start to raise the rod behind you with a slight acceleration, keeping the controlling arm straight. Most of this cast comes from the arm movement at the shoulder.

The rod tip comes forward, traveling pretty flat and with
a slight acceleration.

The rod drops down in front of you, but no lower than head height, still accelerating.

The fastest part of the cast. The rod is traveling back
behind you, staying flat at head height.

Finally, the rod kicks back to the 1 o'clock position, throwing the belly behind you. At this point you wait until the fly line touches the water (splash and go), and then start the forward cast.

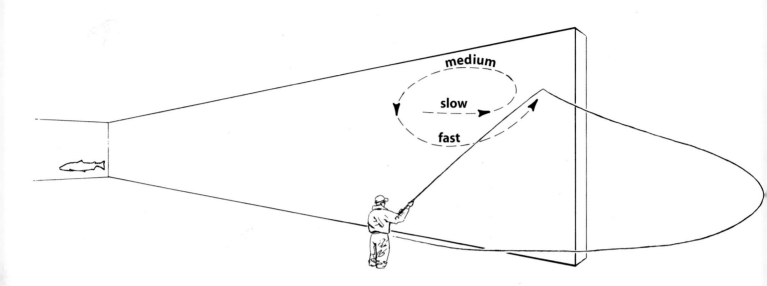

It can help to picture the rod tip drawing the **e** shape along a brick wall that runs 90 degrees to the target off your downstream shoulder. Keep the rod tip on the wall, as far away from you as possible, throughout the cast.

Once you have finished the backstroke and formed the belly behind the rod, you should have rocked all your weight on the back foot (the right foot). It is then a simple matter of finishing off with the forward stroke. Remember that timing is, as always, vital. The backstroke makes all the fly line lift completely out of the water and land again parallel to the target. The forward stroke is similar in timing to the single spey—splash and go! The moment that the first piece of fly line touches the water you must start the forward stroke.

The next group of photos will show you how the cast should look with the fly line out. I have switched to the left bank so that these photos are a left-handed snake roll. With the left hand up, the snake roll is actually a reverse **e** shape—clockwise in direction.

The line starts on the dangle, and the rod points directly downstream, level with your hat.

After drawing the rod tip backward, keeping it level,
accelerate the rod up and forward, lifting the fly line up
and out of the water.

Pull the rod back low with a good acceleration. Only now does the fly line leave the water from the dangle, forming a large loop in front.

The rod comes back toward 1 o'clock with all the fly line
airborne.

Hold the rod still at 1 o'clock, and wait for the line to touch (splash and go). Note that the rod is held away from the body and the belly, the rod, and the fly line are all in perfect alignment.

The fly line has just touched the water and the forward
cast starts.

Loop outbound.

Initially it doesn't matter where the nail knot lands on the backcast of the snake roll. In this case the anchor is well in front of the caster, resulting in a small belly. This is great when there is little room behind you, but when there is plenty of space, try for a bigger belly.

Initially you should practice this cast in two parts, working on getting the backstroke right before worrying about timing and forward stroke. To get it right, the fly and line must jump out the water from the dangle and land dead straight in front of you and parallel to the target. As you get more accomplished at the backstroke, start to watch the anchor point at the end of the fly line. To start, it will be somewhere in front of you—maybe 20 feet

or so. As you get better and develop more control of this stage of the cast, you should try to get the end of the line to land directly downstream of you—in your wading wake, though still facing the target.

Practice with different shapes, sizes, and speeds of the e to see the results you get. Remember that flat is good, and the better you get, the flatter and more compressed your e will be.

The best cast and the biggest belly always result from pulling the anchor point back far enough so that it lands downstream of you and in your wading wake.

A weak or small **e** shape results in the fly line staying anchored in the water much too far downstream.

THE 5 MOST COMMON ERRORS

1. **Problem:** The line tip stays in the water throughout the e shape.

    Cause: Too slow (or small) an e shape.

2. **Problem:** The fly or line hits the rod in mid-e.

    Cause: Not being fast enough on the underside of the e shape to pull the rod out of the way, by pausing slightly while drawing the e instead of keeping it one continuous movement, or by drawing the whole e off the brick wall and more over your head.

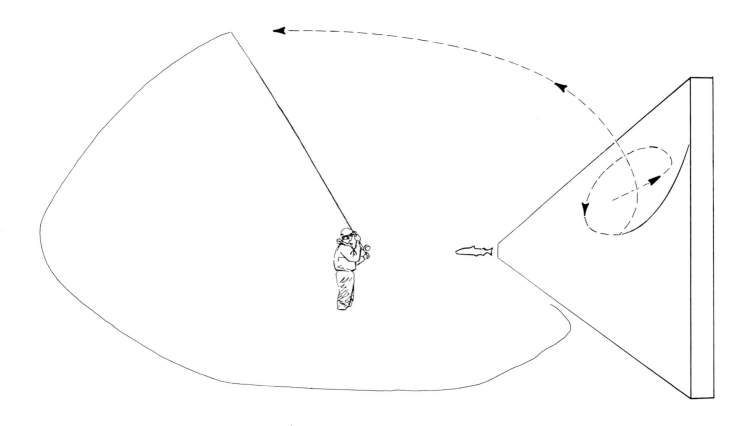

If the rod tip leaves the wall at the end of the backcast, it will hook the belly behind you and the line will hit you on the forward stroke, pulling the belly off course from the 180-degree plane. This is very common.

3. **Problem:** The fly line lands on the water at the end of the backstroke not aligned and parallel to the target.

Cause: This is usually caused by not having your brick wall at 90 degrees to your target.

4. **Problem:** The fly bounces out of the water on the backstroke behind you and into the bushes (or does not even touch the water).

Cause: Usually this is caused by too much speed on the lift of the rod tip from the end of the e to 1 o'clock.

Many casters have a tendency to hook the rod too far around the back of the head (like a golf swing), pulling the belly behind. The belly will hit the caster on the forward cast. This cast looks like it is nicely lined up to cast at a fine angle downstream; however, the anchor is facing across the river.

5. **Problem:** Hooking the belly around the back of your head too much and hitting yourself on the head with the fly line during the forward stroke.

   Cause: The rod tip comes away from the brick wall once it has lifted to 1 o'clock and drifts behind you. Keep the rod tip away from your body!

Things to think about when practicing the snake roll cast:

1. Start with 45 to 55 feet of line washed tight downstream and the rod raised level with your hat.

2. Draw the e shape—clockwise with the left hand and counterclockwise with the right—and lift the rod to 1 o'clock directly opposite your target.

3. Keep the rod held away from you and along the brick wall.

4. Wait for the fly line tip to touch the water.

5. Drive the forward cast out near to the line lying on the water in front of you.

CHAPTER 12

The Circle Spey and Snap T

BACKGROUND

There are two distinct forms of the snap T. The first uses soft curves of the rod tip and produces controlled backcasts; the second is much more aggressive and involves vertical waves of the rod. There is some debate over the name of each version. Many call the first version the circle spey or snap C, and the second version the snap T. My personal preference is the first version, which I have always known as the snap T. This is the name I will use for the cast in this chapter. In any case, both casts are very similar bar the opening moves.

The snap T is the newest in the family of spey casts. I first saw it demonstrated in the United Kingdom when a bunch of English spey bums got together to throw some line, chew the breeze, and live the spey life! It was introduced to me as the Coxon kick—named after one of the great modern English spey casters, Gary Coxon. Very soon after that I was shown it in detail by my spey bro, Jim Vincent. He called it the snap T and said that it was a favorite cast of the Sunk Line Steelheaders of the West Coast. It certainly makes light work of getting up a deeply sunk tip, and I would recommend it for those who do have problems casting a sink tip with the single spey. It is an easy cast to learn, much easier in fact than the single spey, and because it is used in the same situations as the single spey, a great alternative to trying to learn this tricky cast.

Why use it? Change of direction, with long line, obstacles behind.
When to use it? Upstream wind.
Which hand to use? Left hand up on the right bank of the river. Right hand up on the left bank.
Group? Waterborne anchor.

Another use of the snap T is when you are fishing more than one fly. If you fish droppers a lot and use the single spey, you will quite often get tangles. This is because the anchor point with the single spey is more prone to landing in a bit of a heap, tangling your flies together. With the snap T, you tend to get a much straighter anchor point and, therefore, fewer tangles with a dropper on.

I started to teach the snap T in the summer of 2000. I was teaching for a company called Sportfish, at their new facility near Reading in England, and the standard lesson was for one hour. In that short time I found it very hard to give clients a good understanding of the single spey—and impossible to teach the complete beginner. The snap T gives clients a very fishable cast in a short time.

I know the snap T is not a classic spey, but for saving me hours of frustration and pressure, I give it a vote into the spey-cast hall of fame.

Start with the rod tip pointing downstream and slowly lift the rod straight up *(1)*. At the top of the lift, sweep the rod toward the middle of the river *(2)*, and then drop it down toward the surface *(3)* and accelerate back toward the near bank *(4)*. The whole move makes a large **D**.

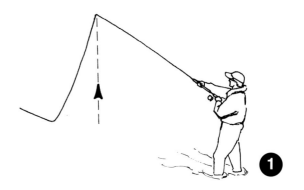

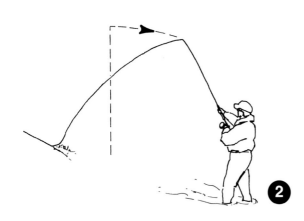

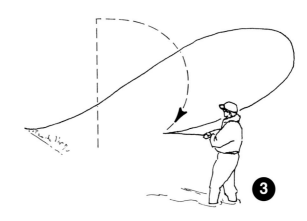

Start the snap T with a slow lift of the rod, which is pointing directly downstream about a foot off the surface (the bottom left corner of the **D**).

HOW TO

As in all the other casts, this is described for a right-handed caster. You are standing on the left bank of the river, the line is on the dangle, and you want to cast your fly back across the river at an angle of 60 degrees or so. Stand with your left foot forward (weight mostly on this foot), angled toward the target, and your body facing your target. Again, draw the imaginary orange line on the water, directly between your front foot and your target. For the snap T, you will draw a very large letter D with your rod tip.

Imagine you are in a room with four walls; you are standing in the middle of the room facing the front wall. The correct D shape should be drawn on the left side wall (for the right-handed cast), not the front wall.

Continue the lift until the rod tip is at about 11 o'clock, still pointing downstream, making the vertical part of the **D**.

The rod pushes out toward the far bank, even with your body.

The rod suddenly accelerates down toward the water and in toward the bank with a snap, traveling fast, flat, and low.

The rod stops low, pointing downstream and slightly behind you, while the fly line shoots upstream past you.

Patience is needed here: Point the rod downstream while all the fly line zips past and lands on the water. Wait with your rod tip at the end of the **D** until the line tip and fly land on the water. Only then does stage 2 start.

Stage 2 starts with the rod traveling quite flat across your body, chasing the fly line.

white mouse

There needs to be enough speed in the rod tip for the white mouse to start. The rod is still traveling upstream and keeping quite flat.

When the rod has passed your upstream shoulder, lift it to 1 o'clock, rocking lightly onto your back foot, and wait for the belly to pull tight and the white mouse to reach the nail knot. As always, when the rod is at 1 o'clock, it should be directly opposite your target—the 180-degree principle. If done correctly, you will move all the fly line on the water from a position facing downstream— pirouetting the very tip of the fly line—and align it with your target on the forward stroke.

After the belly has tightened the forward cast starts. Bear
in mind one point: The timing with the snap T is a little
different from the rest of the spey casts. This cast has the
longest pause of all between the end of the backstroke
and the start of the forward stroke.

A good forward cast unrolls completely in the air before landing on the water.

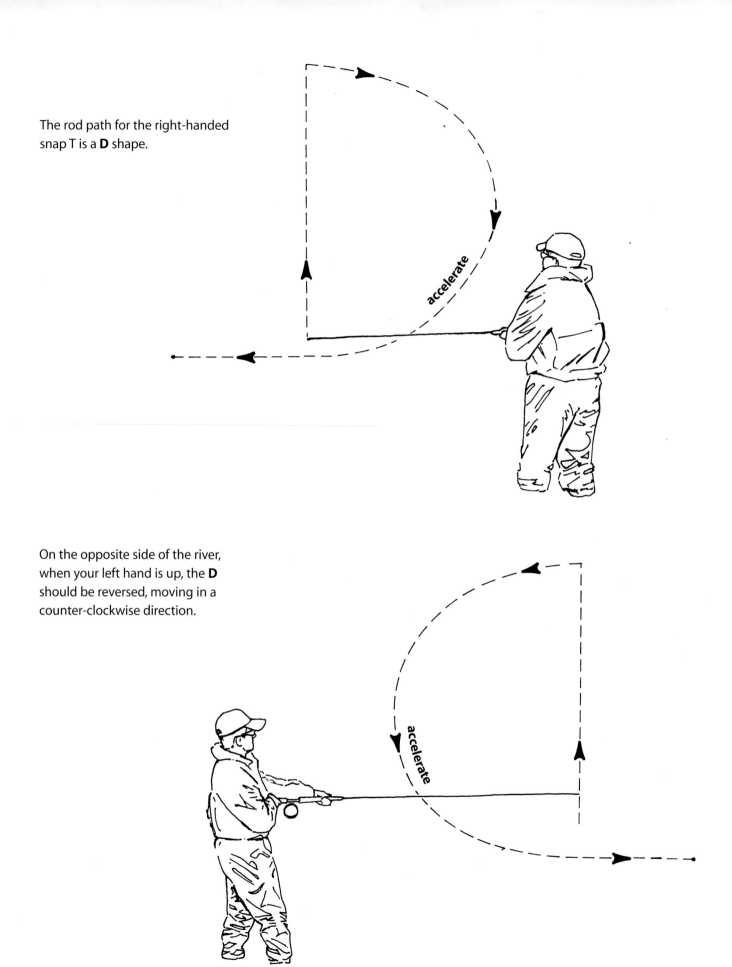

The rod path for the right-handed snap T is a **D** shape.

On the opposite side of the river, when your left hand is up, the **D** should be reversed, moving in a counter-clockwise direction.

accelerate

accelerate

With the left hand up, the snap T is reversed—a **C** instead of a **D**. As before, start with the rod pointing downstream and raise the rod.

Push the rod tip up and across toward the middle of the
river.

Smoothly drop the rod down to about chin level and then accelerate the rod flat back toward the bank while keeping it low.

Wait in this position until all the line lands, and then
finish off with stage 2 and the forward cast.

Too weak or small a **D** and an ineffective snap make all the line stay downstream of you.

THE 5 MOST COMMON ERRORS

1. **Problem:** The tip of the fly line and the fly stay stuck in the water downstream of you and the orange line after the snap.

   Cause: Drawing the D too small or not snapping the lower part hard or flat enough.

Too big a **D** or drawing the **D** too far across the river and not on a downstream plane results in the tip of the line flying way upstream of you.

2. **Problem:** Throwing the fly and fly line tip too far upstream of you. Ideally it should land just about opposite where you are standing.

Cause: The most likely cause of this is by drawing the D shape in a plane too far across the river and not far enough downstream. It can also be caused if you have too much curve on the D or move the rod too fast when drawing the upper part of the curve. The fly will then land 20 to 30 feet upstream of you. When you start the chase with the fly so far upstream, you cannot avoid the bloody L.

Too slow a stage 2 or the dreaded dip cause the bloody L.

3. **Problem:** The bloody L.

   Cause: Chasing the rod too slowly on stage 2 or doing the dreaded dip. It can also be caused by throwing the fly too far upstream as in problem 2.

4. **Problem:** Lifting the fly out of the water during stage 2.

   Cause: Sweeping the rod too fast or too steep on the chase.

5. **Problem:** Having no load at the start of the forward cast.

   Cause: There are a couple of reasons for this. Probably the most common is not pausing long enough at the end of stage 2. When practicing with yarn, or nothing on the end of the line, this will result in a crisp, whip-crack noise. When doing this with a fly, you can easily crack off the fly, so avoid it! The other likely reason for no load is that the D loop is not 180 degrees from the forward cast.

Things to think about when practicing the snap T cast:

1. Start with a tight line, washed downstream and the rod low, pointing 4 feet toward the river.

2. Draw a D shape (clockwise) with the right hand and a C shape (counterclockwise) with the left.

3. Chase the rod low and accelerate as you lift to 1 o'clock, directly opposite your target.

4. Wait for the belly to form.

5. Drive the forward cast out near the line lying on the water in front of you.

As I mentioned at the beginning of this chapter, there are two distinct forms of the snap T. The version I have described (with the D and C) is the way that has worked best for me as a caster and as an instructor. This, I feel, is a better way of being accurate with the snap—and a way to avoid cracking off your fly when using a 400-grain sink tip. The other way of doing the snap T involves more of a vertical wave of the rod. You start the rod pointing downstream with the line washed tight, then lift the rod smoothly up to about 11 o'clock (still pointing directly downstream), and without any pause, flick the rod tip back down toward the water and slightly in toward your bank. This (done correctly) results in the fly jumping out of the water and traveling past you to land in the water again, above your orange line. Once it has landed, the cast is finished off in the same way as described earlier. To distinguish the two forms of the cast, some people call this vertical version the snap T and the version I described as the snap C or circle spey. To avoid confusion, I have kept calling this cast the snap T.

I am not a fan of the vertical way of doing the snap T as the line can come back at lightning speed when you don't know how to judge it correctly. This is not only dangerous, but with very heavy tips and heads on, the line speed will crack off a fly. I have seen this often. However, as in all casting, try out both ways and find the one that works best for you.

CHAPTER 13

The Devon Switch

BACKGROUND

I debated long and hard whether to include this cast in a book on spey casting, as it is not a spey cast in the true sense. However, having included the overhead cast, I decided to add this one as well. My father taught me it back in the '70s when he had his fly-fishing school and was teaching me how to cast and teach. I don't know much about its history and when it was first used, but I do know there are a number of situations where this cast has proved its worth.

It is a useful cast, particularly for beginners, and was a cast I used to use a lot, before I became so enamored with the spey casts. Actually, there is a time and a place for this cast, particularly for the single-handed rod caster. I used to teach students this cast for night fly fishing for sea trout. In the daytime, there is no problem in making a spey cast, but at night, when sea trout fishing, it is too dark to clearly see the anchor point of a spey cast. This can result in poor timing, as well as not knowing where your anchor is, and making the fatal mistake of crossing the anchor on the forward cast, resulting in a tangle. A tangle at night can be disastrous to the rest of the night's sport, as the flashlight has to go on and the pool spooked for a length of time. Evenings of tangles often resulted in finishing off the night's sport in the Black Horse in Torrington or the Rising Sun at Umberleigh, quaffing quantities of ale, and talking about how good the fishing could have been!

Why use it? Medium line length, obstacles behind, change of direction.

When to use it? An alternative to the single spey. Its best use is at night, when the spey caster cannot see the anchor.

Which hand to use? Right hand up off the left bank, left hand up off the right bank.

HOW TO

As ever, make sure the line is lying taut on the water and mostly pointing downstream on the dangle. Start with about 40 to 50 feet. The cast is quite similar to the single spey, though with no anchor. Start with the same grip and stance—right hand up off of the left bank and left foot forward. Start the rod tip low, very low—about 4 inches above the water surface and pointing directly down the line.

The backcast, as such, is made with the rod drawing a letter J. You can change direction as much as 90 degrees with this cast, though the more angle change you make, the more you should accelerate and the more emphasis there is on the speed of the hook shape. Also, you need to pause longer to give the line time to drift farther behind you, and you need more room behind you than if you were only changing direction by 45 degrees or so.

The rod starts low on the dangle *(1)* and then sweeps upstream rapidly, hooking into a **J** shape *(2)*. The straight part of the sweep—in front of you—should stay quite low, only lifting once the rod is upstream of your shoulders. The movement throws the fly line mostly upstream with enough side momentum to hook a few feet of line behind you, which loads the rod. A brief pause for the backcast to tighten, and then the forward cast begins *(3)*.

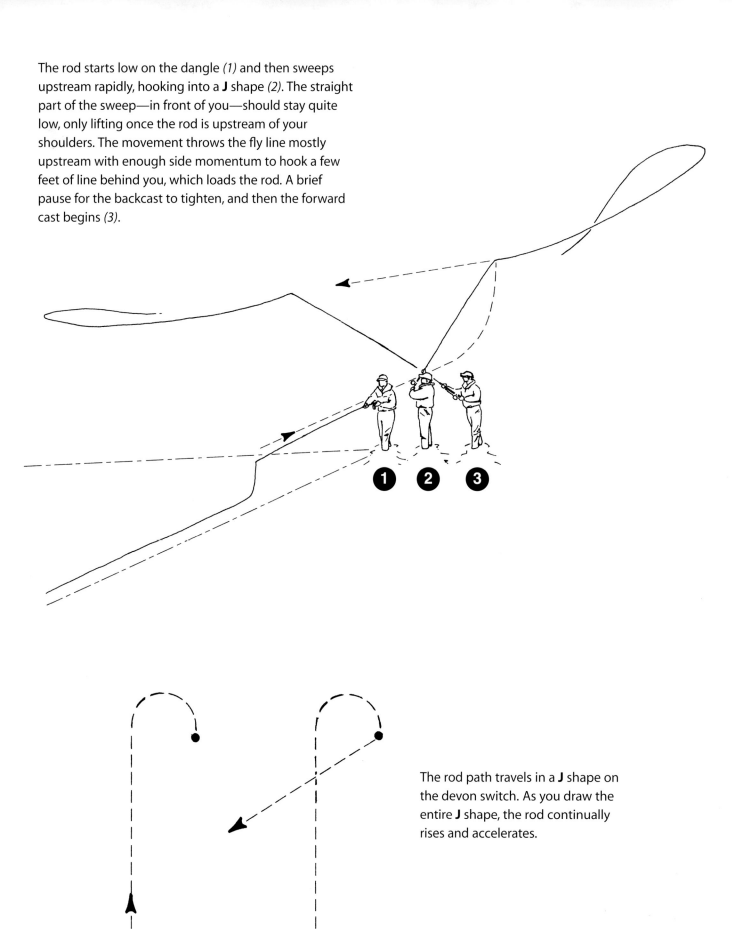

The rod path travels in a **J** shape on the devon switch. As you draw the entire **J** shape, the rod continually rises and accelerates.

The rod starts very low to the water and pointing directly down the fly line. The straight part of the **J** is drawn with the rod across your body, starting from the low position (4 inches above the water) and then accelerating upstream while rising slightly.

At the end of the backstroke, the rod is at 1 o'clock and opposite the target; pause while the fly line travels mostly directly upstream and high. Notice how the fly line is traveling upstream rather than behind the caster.

Without pausing or slowing the rod, draw the hook part of the **J** behind you and up to 1 o'clock behind you. The momentum should be mostly upstream, which takes the fly line upstream, but the hook part of the cast drifts some of the fly line behind you. This is enough line to load the rod as the forward cast starts. The fly line and fly go behind you only 15 feet or so.

The forward cast starts when the rod is loaded, since there is no anchor point.

This is a cast that isn't very effective with a long line outside the rod as it takes tremendous speed for the fly line to travel upstream and also drift behind the rod enough to load it. However, with a medium or short belly length line this cast works very well and is capable of throwing over 100 feet with only a rod length of room behind you.

As I mentioned earlier, this cast is particularly useful for night fishing when you cannot see your anchor point with a spey cast. It is also a very fast way to change direction between 45 and 90 degrees when you are speed fishing, particularly if you haven't yet mastered the single spey cast. Finally, the devon switch is most useful when fishing a dry fly with obstructions behind, as there is no anchor point to get the dry fly wet.

This is quite a good cast with a single-handed rod and less useful with the two-handed rod. The length and diameter of the two-handed rods means there is a lot of air resistance on the rod as you draw the fast J shape, making it a cast that uses too much effort in my opinion to be a regularly used cast. With a single-handed rod, it's a different story!

THE 5 MOST COMMON ERRORS

1. **Problem:** Unable to get the line out of the water on the backstroke.

   Cause: The rod sweeps too flat or too slow on the I part of the J.

2. **Problem:** The fly line touches the water on the backstroke.

   Cause: The rod has dipped on the backcast, or you have paused too long before starting the forward cast.

3. **Problem:** No load or tension on the rod as the forward cast starts.

   Cause: Not enough speed on the hook part of the cast to get enough line behind the caster to load the rod.

4. **Problem:** The fly line goes too far behind you and hooks the bushes.

   Cause: Too much speed on the hook part of the cast and not enough speed on the upstream I.

5. **Problem:** Hitting the rod tip or tangling in the fly line on the forward cast.

   Cause: The rear loop is thrown too far upstream for the angle of the forward cast. Either aim the forward cast more downstream or put more speed in the hook part of the backstroke so there is some line behind the rod to load it and get a straight 180-degree pull.

Things to think about when practicing the devon switch cast:

1. Start with a tight line and the rod low, pointing directly down the fly line.

2. Sweep the rod to the side, rising constantly and accelerating in a J shape to 1 o'clock behind you and opposite your target.

3. Wait for the fly line tip to tighten on the backcast and slightly curl behind you.

4. Smoothly accelerate the forward cast out, driving the rod in a straight line.

CHAPTER 14

Advanced Spey Casting

So far, this book has been concentrating on the basics of spey casting. The idea has been to give you an introduction into the family of spey casts and to enable most casters to cope with a given situation.

Real students of spey casting need to know a few extra things to help achieve great distances of the cast. It takes a great deal of precision and control to master these advanced techniques. I realize that most casters who read this book may not be skilled enough to move to the advanced casts. If you don't think you are ready, do not try these casts. I'd hate for your casting to go horribly wrong!

BELLY CONTROL

Most of the advanced techniques in spey casting require control of the belly. Remember, this is the part of the cast that loads the rod and gives an efficient forward cast. The more the rod loads, the faster the line speed, the less effort needed, and the better the end result. In advanced casting techniques, there are three essential differences in the belly: the size, the shape, and the speed.

Belly Size

A big belly loads the rod more than a little belly. Here lies one of the anomalies of the cast. The spey cast is used when there are obstructions behind you, yet I have been saying all along that the bigger the belly, the better. A good spey caster needs to be able to control the size of the belly according to the space behind. When there is room, throw the belly back 30 feet and stroke the forward cast out against this mass. When tight to the trees, deliberately throw a small belly behind, but with so little line weight to load the rod, the forward stroke must be powerful. This skill is only achieved by practice. Think again of our friend the golfer. He is on the putting green and has to be able to putt the ball consistently 5 feet (not $5^{1}/_{2}$), but he also needs to be able to putt exactly 30 feet consistently. This degree of skill is attained by the top golfers, and likewise, only the top spey casters can throw back a belly exactly how far they want.

The true master of spey casting pushes the belly as far back as he can. In this case the belly is using over 50 feet of line to load the rod. The belly, rod tip, and anchor are precisely lined up: a perfect example of the 180-degree principle. The caster has paused too long here for the cast to succeed in order to show the degree of alignment a cast should have.

Throwing too large a belly when you are close to bushes, though, can create problems.

A good spey caster adjusts the belly size according to how much room there is. When you are this tight to the bushes, you need a very small belly.

A traditional belly is rounded and open. Though it may be large, it will have less line speed as it goes backward and load the rod a lot less than the V loop.

Belly Shape

Here is a subject that is rarely talked about in spey casting, though it is an important point that most casters recognize with an overhead cast. In the overhead cast, a tight loop is considered the perfect end result, and a wedge, or arrow-pointed loop has more penetration than a curved or rounded loop. All the best casters can throw these arrow-pointed loops.

Spey casting is no different, though in this case, the key factor is the shape of the belly. Another term for the belly is the D loop. This is a good name, because it creates a clear picture of the line shape and how it should look at the end of the backstroke. Whether you call it the belly or the D loop, there is

one problem with this rounded shape. It has a lot of air resistance in the backcast, slowing the line speed down and giving a somewhat passive load to the rod. At the advanced level what you are trying to achieve is a V loop. The ideal shape of the belly behind you is >. With a belly this shape, there is more backward pull against the rod than with a D shape (because of the decrease in air resistance), and even with a belly of the same size, it is a better-loading and more aggressive belly to load the rod.

A perfect belly for the advanced spey caster should be a **V** or wedge shape. There is so much line speed, as well as mass, in this belly that the forward cast is effortless.

You make all the same moves in the advanced single spey as with the standard single spey, though the lifts and dips are much flatter. Start the rod pointing slightly across the river and raise it up only as far as 10 o'clock.

To get these V loops you need to think what causes a tight loop with an overhead cast. Short, positive stops of the rod, a rod tip traveling in as horizontal plane as possible and a fast tip action rod! Forming a tight, arrow-pointed belly requires the same stipulations.

Without a pause, start the back sweep, keeping the rod traveling as flat as possible. It must still have a dip at the very top of the lift, but this is much more subtle in the advanced casts. Note how much bend there is in the rod at this stage.

Turn at the knees and hips, the rod still traveling flat and fast. The line is completely airborne, and the rod fully flexed.

The rod is now back opposite the target and the line, still airborne, is coming upstream and behind you, still very low. By lifting the rod to 1 o'clock, the belly would open up into a big **D** shape with lots of air resistance. Keeping it this low results in the wedge shape.

Keep the rod still until the line tip anchors, and then start the forward cast.

Outbound!

I stress the importance of finishing the backcast with a rod lift, regardless of which spey cast you are performing. While this is a very important tip for the beginner to observe, the more advanced caster needs to be wary of this. At the end of the backcast, the more the rod lifts, the more it pulls open the rear belly. You can form a very small, tight V loop behind you, but you pull it into a large, rounded D loop by lifting the rod tip up to 1 o'clock. This takes out the line speed of the D loop and only gives you the benefit of the mass of the belly. So, in summary:

1. Use a fast tip action rod.

2. When throwing the belly back behind you, don't drift to a stop with the rod—stop the rod positively.

3. Keep the rod tip traveling as horizontal as possible when throwing the belly behind. Avoid the big figure-eight movements that are so often described and associated with the spey casts— and remember, flat is good!

Belly Speed
The last factor that really helps the rod to load is the speed that the belly is traveling backwards, or more accurately, the energy that the line has when the forward cast starts. This is effected by its shape, as previously mentioned, but also by how fast you throw the rod backwards. What you are trying to end up with is an aggressive belly, not a passive belly.

The belly is going to travel behind you, say, 10 feet. A passive belly is a belly that travels only 10 feet behind the rod, slowing down as it travels back before losing most of its kinetic energy. As you start the forward cast against 10 feet of motionless weight, the rod will load and the forward cast goes out. However, if you throw the belly back 10 feet, yet it has enough speed to go back 20 feet, you now have an aggressive belly. It is still only 10 feet in size, but you are driving forward against the line's kinetic energy as well as its potential. The results can be fantastic and make big-distance spey casting very effortless.

This is not as hard as it sounds to get right. At the start of a spey cast, the line is held by the water surface tension and this surface tension is what stops the belly from going back cleanly and easily. To get an aggressive belly, start the backstroke of the spey cast with the rod much lower to the water than usual and throw the backstroke back hard, low, and flat. Because the rod starts low, the line will hit and bite into the water earlier, which means you can put this fast backstroke in without losing the anchor point. Try casting backwards with the same speed, only with the rod tip traveling upwards, or even traveling back flat but high, and you will never get an anchor point to stick. The line may touch the water, but the excessive speed means that the anchor will skim off the water surface, like a flat stone skipping over the water surface.

Remember, there is a direct relationship between how low your rod travels and how fast it travels. The lower your rod is to the water the faster it can travel on the belly formation stroke—relying on the low line to grab the water earlier, but needing the speed to initially break the surface tension. As the rod travels back higher, it needs to go slower, to avoid throwing the fly into the bushes behind. "Fast and low" or "high and slow."

To give you an idea, my rod tip starting position (for maximum load and effect) is never higher than my chin on the single spey and switch casts. It is from this starting position that I begin to form the belly. With the double spey I don't worry about the starting position so much, but when the belly is formed (which is halfway through stage 2), I keep my rod low, flat, and fast.

The same will apply to the snake roll and snap T. Save the energy and apply the power when the rod tip is about to form the belly; then keep the rod tip traveling, flat, fast, and low.

One of the hardest transitions for the caster moving into this advanced style is to avoid lifting the rod to 1 o'clock at the end of the backstroke. Most experts say that this is a good place to stop the rod. While this is true for beginners, advanced casters should get away from this high rod-stopping position. The reason I say this is that any upward movement in the rod at the end of the backstroke opens the loop up and slows the line speed down. You can form a beautiful wedge-shaped back loop, but lifting the rod up to 1 o'clock after forming this loop will round the loop off and take out some of the awesome energy stored in the arrow-shaped loop. For the perfect forward cast, I tend to finish with my rod at 2 o'clock or even half past two.

This is the part where you can really fall down. In most cases, spey casters attempting to finish the rod behind them at the 2 o'clock position will make the backstroke and then drop the rod to 2 o'clock. This is wrong. A falling rod tip at this stage will only result in laying more fly line on the water (more stick) and will take out the extreme tension involved in the line, loading the rod less and making a pig's ear out of the cast. The rod can finish this far back, but it needs to rise to that point, or at least travel back flat to it.

As with all these advanced tips, start the practice with the switch cast, get confident with it, and then move on to the rest of the spey casts.

The belly is where advanced techniques really matter. Of course, perfect casting still requires immaculate timing and a good tight forward loop, so before you attempt to move on to advanced belly control, you should master the forward loop and timing.

ADVANCED DOUBLE SPEY

An aggressive belly is necessary for all advanced spey casts. With the double spey there is yet another change that can make the difference. In stage 2, in most cases, the rod sweeps around from the upstream shoulder to behind you off the downstream shoulder. This sweep creates an energy in the fly line that travels downstream and behind you—

a sideways centrifugal energy. The resulting cast works, but to take it to the next level, you need to focus on getting all the energy of the belly directly opposite the target and loading the rod to the maximum. As the rod travels from the upstream position at the end of stage 1 to the ready position at 1 o'clock behind you (or 2 o'clock if you are getting good!) at the end of stage 2, a flat, inverted V (with the point of the V across the river to the far bank) or wedge-shaped motion will give far more line speed and energy to the backcast than the usual sweeping motion.

Just a quick word of warning. The setup at the beginning of the cast has to be right. If you make the first movement (stage 1) and the fly lands 25 feet below you, you cannot benefit from the V shape. You may put the V shape into stage 2, but because the fly is anchored so far downstream, you will still have a downstream centrifugal belly, rather than the 180-degree belly that is so hot! The perfect place for the tip of the fly line to land at the end of stage 2 is one rod length from you and about 5 or 6 feet out.

The amount of speed and distance you get from this advanced double spey can be incredible. The rod has so much more flex and load than the usual double spey that it becomes a firm favorite of anyone who gets the hang of it. The only thing to be careful of is that you will always get a huge belly behind you, so be warned if you are standing too close to obstructions behind.

With a regular double spey, the centrifugal force built up by the rod as it comes round on stage 2 results in a belly that can be large but is a long way downstream of you.

The advanced double spey uses an inverted **V**- or wedge-shaped path of the rod tip throughout stage 2. This wedge shape results in a far more efficient belly, one that remains close to you with all the energy lined up for the forward cast.

The **V**- or wedge-shaped stroke on stage 2 starts with the rod in the normal position at the end of stage 1—low and pointing upstream.

The out leg, or first leg, of the **V** is a low flick of the rod tip toward the far bank. This sets a loop of slack in the line in front of you and a white mouse running only a short way.

The in leg of the **V** kicks directly behind you, kicking against the initial loop of slack caused by the out leg. This in leg is a slightly harder kick than the out leg— accelerate the rod, keeping it relatively low and flat.

This is the most efficient belly—tight to the caster. The combination of speed on the in leg and the fact that your rod is accelerating directly away from your target gives you a belly of hyper energy and, potentially, the ultimate double spey.

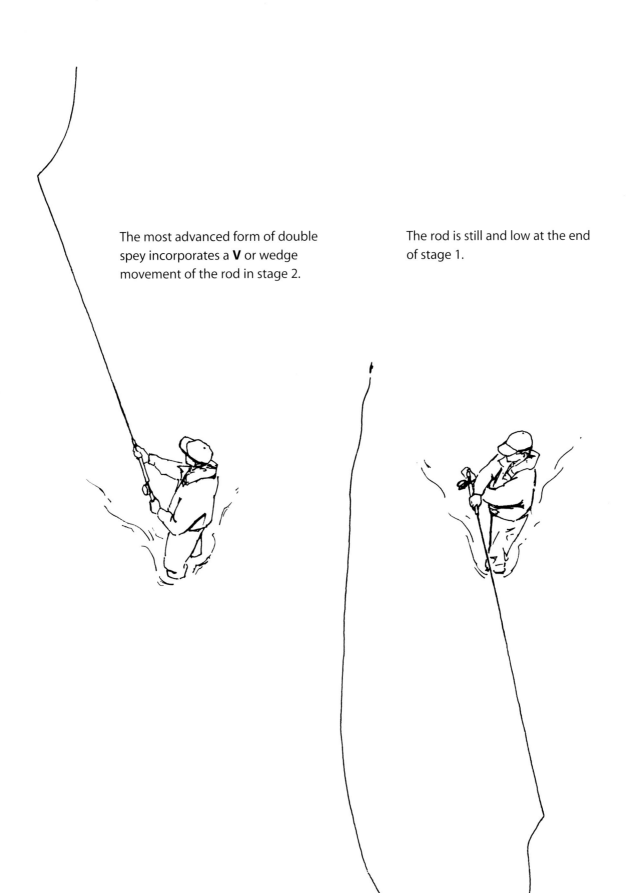

The most advanced form of double spey incorporates a **V** or wedge movement of the rod in stage 2.

The rod is still and low at the end of stage 1.

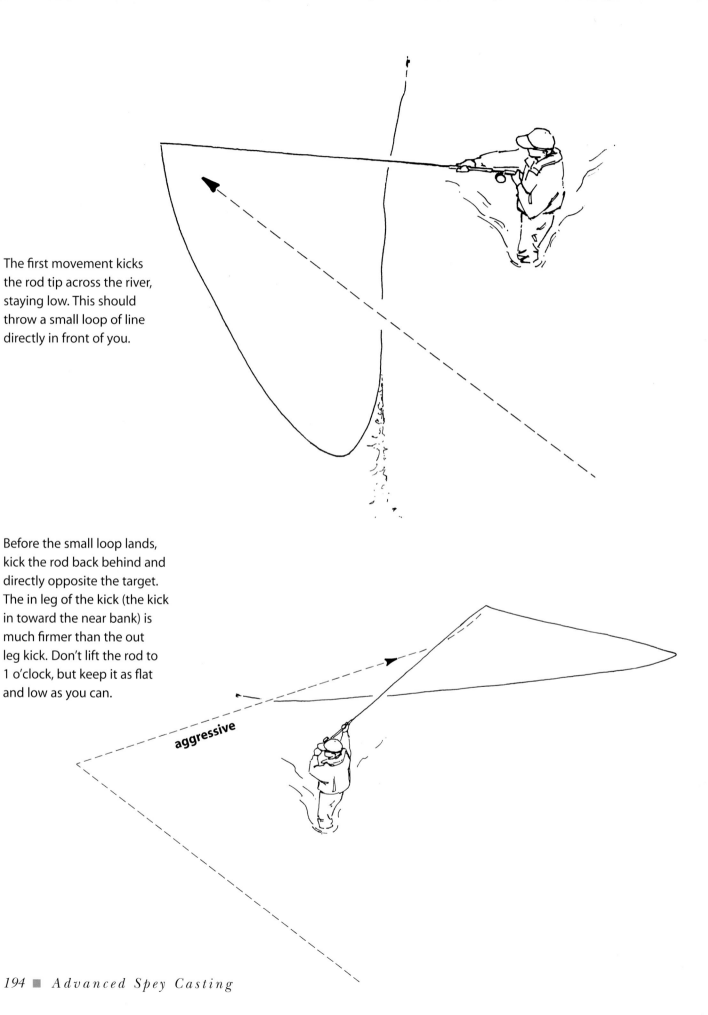

The first movement kicks the rod tip across the river, staying low. This should throw a small loop of line directly in front of you.

Before the small loop lands, kick the rod back behind and directly opposite the target. The in leg of the kick (the kick in toward the near bank) is much firmer than the out leg kick. Don't lift the rod to 1 o'clock, but keep it as flat and low as you can.

aggressive

CHAPTER 15

The Single-Handed Spey Casts

My favorite form of spey casting is with the single-handed rod. Few casters know or use the single-handed rod for spey casting. There are thousands and thousands of competent spey casters with the two-handed rod and a lot of them fish with single-handed rods, but only a few put the two together.

I was brought up in North Devon, in the West Country of England, an area made famous by the books of Henry Williamson—*Tarka the Otter, Salar the Salmon,* and a host of others. The rivers are relatively small, like the Torridge at Torrington, where a cast of twenty yards is about as far as you need. Or the beautiful river Bray at Clapworthy. There the river runs under leafy alders and oaks and the summer run of sea trout, grilse, and occasional salmon make it one of the most wonderful rivers to fish. On the Bray a cast of 20 feet is long. These rivers are lined with trees with many deep pools that make it

A shoal of salmon and sea trout lying in Black Pool on the Bray. This river is much too small to fish with a two-handed rod, making the single-handed spey casts essential.

impossible to wade far out. The only way to fish these pools is with a spey cast, and this is where my love of spey casting was truly kindled.

TACKLE

As with two-handed spey casting, there are two schools on how to spey cast the line out, and your style influences your fly line choice. There are those who like to have a fairly short line and to be able to spey cast it out some distance by shooting line on the forward stroke of the spey cast. For this preference of casting, the perfect fly line has a reasonably short head (35 to 40 feet total) with a short rear taper (2 to 4 feet). To get good distance spey casting with this type of line, you need to keep the whole head outside the rod. When you complete the forward cast, let the thin running line go, and it will shoot some distance. Distance varies with skill level, but a good spey caster should be able to get at least seventy feet shooting line with a weight-forward 5-weight line.

The other way of spey casting a single-handed rod is to have a long-head fly line—traditionally a double taper, or at least a salmon/steelhead taper that has a head length of 60 feet or more and a very long rear taper (20 feet or so). This extra head and taper length makes it much easier to mend the fly line and control the fly. It is also easier to pick up the amount of line you are fishing and spey cast it back out again without having to strip in the running line and have it dangling at your feet. One final advantage that this double taper line (or long belly) has over its shorter-head cousins is that it is more versatile to use with the more complex single-handed spey casts mentioned later in this chapter. I used to like the short-head lines as I could get distance very easily; however, now I am quite passionate for the longer-head lines and rarely, if ever, do I use the short-head lines.

With regard to rods, it's the same as with the two-handed rods: I favor fast and tippy! I love the tight loops and the evenness of the loops that are formed with these faster rods. Maybe for some they are not so good at fishing short distances as the softer rods because they don't load as easily, but for any caster with a degree of skill, the casts made with fast-action rods look so *sexy*.

TURBO SPEYS

A single-handed spey-casting rod differs little from the two-handed rod in technique, timing, and tackle (apart from shorter rods and lighter lines). The one place that it does differ is in the versatility of the cast. For a start, you have a spare hand, one that is holding the line instead of the rod. Most good single-handed rod casters use this hand to accelerate the line with a double haul to gain distance and penetrate wind on the overhead cast. This is also possible and highly satisfying with the spey cast. Put a single haul into the forward stroke of the spey cast and you greatly increase the line speed. I call this the turbo spey. The haul is applied to the forward stroke of the roll cast, switch cast, single and double spey, snake roll, or snap T and makes shooting a long line with a single-handed rod possible. It is quite possible to cast a whole double-taper 5-weight line down a pool with a 9-foot rod and a limited backcast. How many other casts have that potential?

To get even greater distance, you do a sort of double haul, though you have to be careful with the back haul. Too much speed and all the back haul does is help the fly into the nearest tree behind you. Too slow and there is not enough backward line speed to pull the hands together for the forward haul. The result is slack line on the forward stroke and a collapsed cast. The reason for the rear haul is that the rod isn't long enough to pick a long line out of the water on the backstroke. The haul helps generate enough speed for this to happen and get you into the position for the forward cast. However, just like the regular haul, you do need your two hands together at the start of the forward stroke so that you have the full arm length to haul with. To do this, you need to make sure there is enough speed in the backward-traveling belly to tighten the line and pull your two hands together.

Start the turbo spey with the line tight on the dangle and the rod pointing low and slightly across the river. The line is in the left hand and the two hands are close together.

Smoothly lift the rod tip straight up to about 11 o'clock.

Slightly dip the rod and begin the sweep around behind you—keeping the rod tip traveling pretty flat and the two hands still side by side.

Finish with the rod tip raised to 1 o'clock and opposite the target, and wait for the splash and go.

At the start of the forward cast, the two hands should remain side by side.

As soon as the line tip touches, start the forward stroke.
Finish the cast with a good long haul.

Immediately let the line go when the haul has finished, and watch the line shoot out. To get this right and to get the line speed to its full potential, the forward haul must be timed precisely.

The haul needs to be a full-length, smooth pull, not a jabby tweak, to get real distance.

Be prepared to release the line instantly when the haul has finished. To fully master the turbo spey, you need to ensure that the haul with the line hand and the snap of the wrist with the rod hand are perfectly synchronized. If you time these two movements together, you get the desired results and the line will rocket out with enough speed to shoot a good length, too.

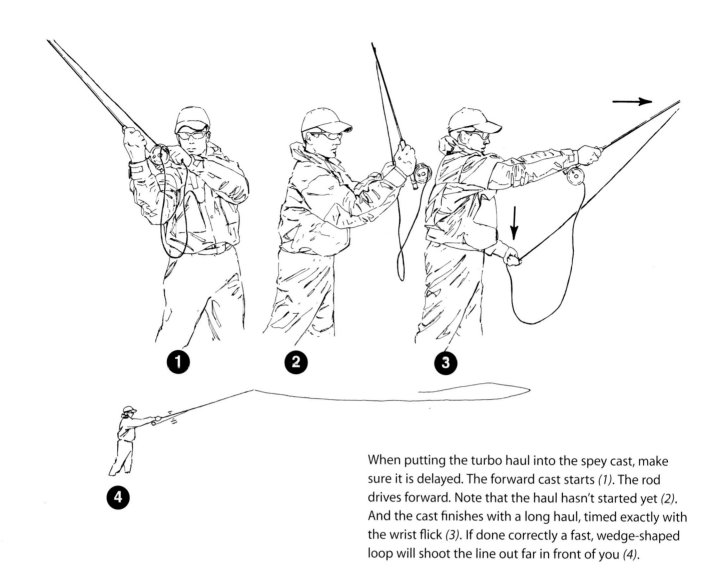

When putting the turbo haul into the spey cast, make sure it is delayed. The forward cast starts *(1)*. The rod drives forward. Note that the haul hasn't started yet *(2)*. And the cast finishes with a long haul, timed exactly with the wrist flick *(3)*. If done correctly a fast, wedge-shaped loop will shoot the line out far in front of you *(4)*.

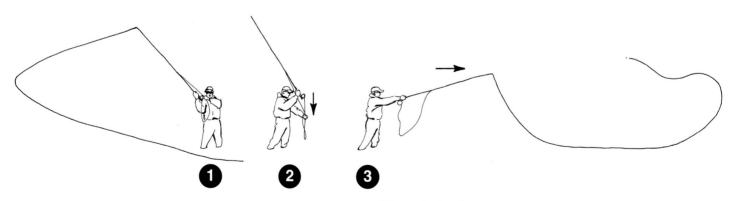

When the haul is timed incorrectly, the line loses speed and power *(1)*. The forward haul has already finished before the rod has started moving *(2)*, and the cast falls into a miserable heap in front of you *(3)*.

The forward haul has started too early, before the rod has started to fire, taking away some of the power and line speed.

Start the dry fly spey by false casting the fly dry directly up and down the river.

DRY FLY SPEY

One more cast that I have used that has a fishing application, though is definitely only for the single-handed rod, I call the dry fly spey. Here's the situation: You are fishing a river and are tucked close into the bank fishing a dry fly. A fish rises across the river from you. You cannot do an overhead cast as you will hook the bush behind you, and you don't want to roll cast or switch cast, as these will drown your dry fly. The solution is the dry fly spey.

After the caster has completed the final forward cast, he immediately dips the rod into the backcast of the single spey. This has to be gentle as there is no water tension to break on the backcast.

The rod waits at 1 o'clock for the line to touch briefly. The leader is higher than the fly line so that only the fly line anchors. The fly stays dry and floats longer.

The anchor splash is small— as soon as the fly line touches the water forward cast starts.

Start the side spey as you would a single spey.

CAST STRINGING

My father gave this name to this type of casting. He also called it the Heineken cast, after the beer and a series of television ads that aired in the '80s. The ads were about a series of impossible feats that could be easily performed after downing a cold Heineken. The punch line in each ad was "only Heineken can do this as it reaches the parts other beers cannot"!

Without the side spey, the river Bray in Devon, England, cannot be easily fished.

Make sure that the rod doesn't lift too high and that the dip remains low as the rod comes around on the backstroke. At the end of the backstroke, the rod should be completely flat and parallel to the water but, as always, directly opposite where you intend the forward cast to go.

My father liked the idea that only Heineken casts can reach the fish other casts cannot!

Cast stringing is where you string together parts of one cast with parts of another to create a new cast that isn't a recognized cast. For example, if there is a tree behind you, you would normally use a spey cast to get the line out. If there is an overhanging tree in front of you, you would use a side cast to keep the fly low and get under the branch. When you have both trees behind and an overhanging tree in front, neither the spey cast nor the side cast works. However, if you string the two casts together you will get a spey cast delivered on a horizontal plane to get underneath the overhanging tree! This is a cast I call the side spey, and it is very useful on small rivers like the Bray.

Wait with the rod still in a horizontal plane until the anchor lands.

Drive the forward cast out sideways and use the haul to help break the water surface tension. Without the haul, it is very difficult to get enough line speed to break the surface meniscus while keeping a very low loop.

The loop travels out sideways and very low. This is a
superb cast for getting underneath an overhanging
branch with no room to backcast.

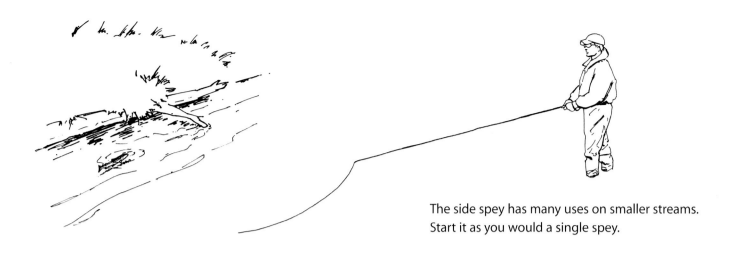

The side spey has many uses on smaller streams. Start it as you would a single spey.

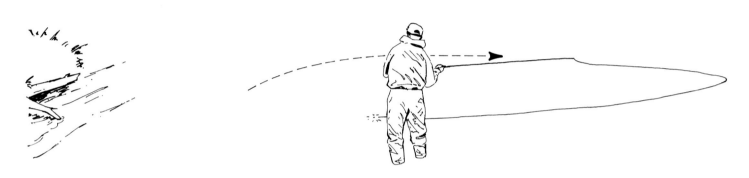

Stop the backcast completely flat and directly opposite the target. As soon as the anchor lands, start the forward stroke.

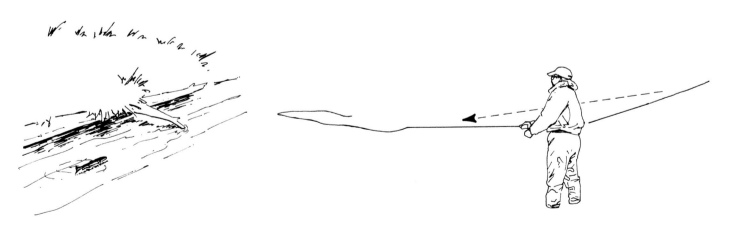

The completely flat side stroke sends out a low horizontal loop, ideal for putting the fly underneath an overhanging tree.

There are an unlimited number of casts you can create by cast stringing. The possibilities are endless. We used a turbo double spey with a side cast and an aerial mend (stringing together four different casts to create a new one) in a particular spot on one of the beats we fished on the Torridge. We used to teach these casts on our annual advanced casting course in our fly-fishing school in Devon. At one of the earliest advanced casting courses we ran, there was a gentleman by the name of Jack, an elderly fly fisher with a good casting foundation and quick to learn. After showing him this quadruple cast string, he performed it to perfection in the aforementioned pool and caught a beautiful sea trout. From then on the pool was known as Jack's Bay.

Here is a list of some of the known spey casts that you can do with a single-handed rod. You can't put them all together, but by playing and practicing, you will soon get to know which casts can go together and which casts cannot.

Basic Casts

Roll Cast	Switch Cast
Single Spey	Double Spey
Snake Roll	Snap T
Devon Switch	Side Cast

Add-ons

Aerial Mend	Reach Mend
Parachute Cast	Shepherd's Crook Cast
Tuck Mend	Double Haul
Nymph Pitch Cast	Slack Line Cast
Single Haul	Pile Cast
Dump Cast	

At the last count, I think I could do 110 different casts with the single-handed rod—stringing together numerous casts from the above lists. A few of them are pretty useless in terms of catching fish, but the majority have a place on some river to get me out of a problem and get my fly to a fish that no one else could reach.

The first step is to realize that these casts are possible and then to get down to the river, string up a 9-foot rod with a double taper or steelhead taper fly line and go to it.

Have fun stringing!

CHAPTER 16

Underhand Casting

One type of spey casting that is getting more popular is the use of shooting heads. Shooting heads are easy to cast. They are short in length, (35 to 45 feet) and attached to a thin shooting line that makes it easy to shoot a long distance with relative ease.

One of Sweden's finest casters, Goran Anderson, has developed a form of spey casting he calls the underhand cast. It is a spey cast, though a different way of doing a spey cast than the traditional style. It is more of a switch cast. It is particular to shooting heads and works very well, potentially getting big distance with little effort.

The advantage of underhand casting is in how little effort it takes to make the cast, and this is achieved by a number of changes to the regular spey cast.

With regular spey casting, you are trying to get the line tip to anchor on the water surface, with the length of line anchor in a direct ratio to the length of line cast. The more fly line out, the more anchor it needs. With the underhand cast, the amount of fly line outside the rod is so short that it doesn't need the anchor. Instead, the leader is the anchor. This means there is less drag to overcome on the forward cast. The leader is thinner and lighter than the fly line, so less energy is lost on the stroke. Because the leader is the anchor, you do need a longer leader than in most spey casting situations. Something between 15 and 18 feet is about right.

Another reason that the underhand is an effortless style of casting is the shortness of the shooting head. There isn't really a set length that the head should be, and it is usually cut to length for different fishing situations. When there is room, the head might be 44 to 46 feet long. As you get into tighter situations, you cut the head back so you need less backcasting room. In some situations, you may end up with a head of only 32 feet. It is an easy way to get the line out when you have virtually no casting space. Just remember, though, if you are cutting a head from 44 feet to 32 feet you are going to lose a lot of the weight that loads the rod, so remember to step up a line size or two, before cutting the head back.

The short head is so easy to pick up and place in the right anchor position that the casting stroke is minimal and efficient. Most casters going from regular spey casting to underhand make too long a stroke with too much power and have difficulty in placing the anchor. Remember, this is an effortless way of casting, and the line is simply steered into position with a short, gentle stroke.

The technique of the underhand cast is not much different from the modern style of spey casting. As with the modern style, you should use a fast-action rod and short, efficient casting strokes, getting the forward loop to unroll in the air like a regular overhead cast. The rod tip doesn't make big dips and swoops like the traditional spey casts, and there is a lot of emphasis on the use of the bottom hand, more so than in the style of spey casting I have been describing.

To begin the underhand cast, point the rod mostly downstream and lift it to about 11 o'clock.

I have found a few problems with this style of casting. First, the recommended grip is with the two hands close together, either side of the reel. This is so the top hand can act as a fulcrum and let the bottom hand make all the power strokes. The problem I have with this is that it is rare to find the reel balancing the rod so far down, so you are fighting the weight and leverage of the rod. I find I cast this style better with my two hands in their usual place—quite far apart. You may also have problems with the long leader. If you are going to fish heavy tube flies, or flies with lead eyes, you do not want a long leader. I also find this style of casting quite boring, as you have to strip in all the line each time you have com-

Draw the rod back toward the near bank while turning your body to face where you are going. This movement is more like steering the line with the bottom hand, rather than dragging it around with the top.

pleted a cast. If you have 35 feet of line and cast 100 feet, you have to retrieve 65 feet each time to make the next cast. Finally, line management may be an issue. Before you cast, you need to pull in all the shooting line you are going to cast and store it somehow on your fingers. This invariably leads to tangles

and the line jamming in the rod rings on the forward cast as you try to shoot 80 feet of line.

For these reasons, this is not a cast I use for fishing. However, if you are a true spey disciple, you need to know it.

Make sure the backcast is gentle to keep the anchor from skipping out. Wait for the leader to touch the water. Note there is a good 2 feet of shooting line outside the rod tip, which makes it easier to control the anchor point.

Start the forward cast. The forward cast power comes almost exclusively from the bottom hand; the top hand is only a pivot point. The rod tip stops high at about 11 o'clock. Note how long the leader is—only the leader is the anchor. You can't see it in the photo, but your bottom hand should stop firmly in your belly button. To help this happen, your upper hand stays bent at the elbow for the entire forward stroke, dropping down instead of driving out.

CHAPTER 17

Left Hand or Right Hand

The biggest safety issue in spey casting is to make sure the line is always on the downwind side of your body as you start the forward cast. This will keep the wind from blowing the line (and fly!) into you. If you are a right-handed caster and the wind is blowing on your right-hand side, it can be very tempting to use only the right hand and try casting off the left shoulder, with the right hand still up. Those who are strongly right-handed will find starting with the left hand up very awkward and clumsy and only through persistent practice will the left-hand approach feel reasonably comfortable. I should know. I was right-hand dominant as a beginning spey caster (and single-handed caster), but then, in the late '80s I forced myself to stick to the left hand. I made myself use it one whole year—whether I was using a salmon rod or single-handed rod, and whether I needed to or not. This was a hard task and a hard year, though gradually I started to improve my left-handed casting and now I am about 80 percent as skilled with my left hand as with my right.

Some casters I have met are naturally ambidextrous and can cast equally well off either arm. These people are rare. Most of us must dedicate ourselves to lots of practice to make the left-handed cast work.

There are plenty of good casters that cast backhanded, or cackhanded in spey casting terms—that is, using the right hand up over the left shoulder

(or left hand up over the right shoulder). This can work for many casters and does present an option when there is a strong wind on the right-hand side. I believe that this is a less effective method than

Some people cast very well backhanded.

225

With a little practice and determination, however, you will have much better results with the left hand.

switching to the left hand up. Body dynamics dictate that you will get better distance, speed, and accuracy without crossing your body with your arms.

It is more a mental battle than a physical one. Most clients I have taught plead against the left hand to start with, saying that they can't use their left hand for anything. Usually I find that they have never even tried the left hand. It takes a little encouragement and some practice before the first reasonable cast goes out. After that, frequently they will say that they cast better left-handed than right-handed. Since there is no ingrained muscle memory to overcome, you have to be more careful with the stroke. That's it; from then on the whole thing starts to become easier and less clumsy!

Try the left hand up with a cast that you are really confident with—like a roll cast. Do a few with the right hand, and then switch hands (and feet!) and try a few with the left hand up. Work with this cast, alternating hands and feet frequently, to become less clumsy. Gradually move on to another of the spey casts until you have some control with both hands on all the casts. Then, *do not forget it*. Every day you fish, put your left hand up for part of the time. Only in this way will you become adept and proficient. And then when you come across a day when you have to use the left hand up, you can!

I apologize to the natural left handers who read this book for not going through the process of the casts with the left hand up.

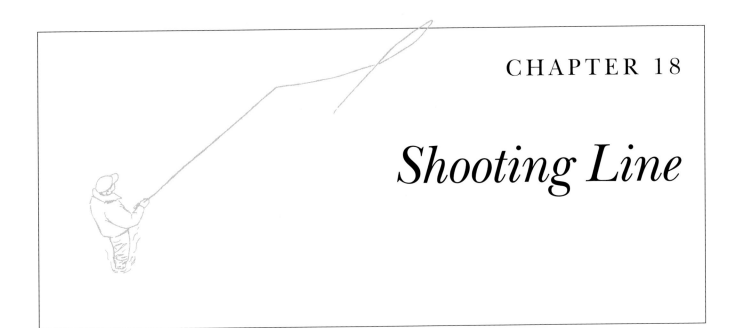

CHAPTER 18

Shooting Line

To get real distance with a spey cast and use minimum effort, you need to shoot some line on the forward cast. You may need to make a few changes to your technique, but it is fairly easy once you are an accomplished spey caster. The main tip is to change the trajectory of the forward cast.

As you get better at spey casting, you can start to increase the power of your forward stroke to get the extra distance needed. For beginners, this is not advised. Most beginners don't have the skill to judge what a cast requires in power and then to increase power to get the extra distance. And I've found nearly all beginners overpower the spey cast anyway. A golf instructor once told me not to try and hit the ball so hard, just let the natural club head speed do the work. As a novice golfer, I couldn't master this subtlety. The pros all seem to wallop the ball as hard as they can! It works for them, why not me? Generally, in spey casting there is a 70/30 ratio. A spey caster should use about 70 percent of the power in creating the backcast and only about 30 percent of power on the forward cast. This changes as you get better and want to shoot longer lengths of line.

An average caster shouldn't expect to shoot more than a few feet of line. As your technique improves, you should be able to shoot a lot more line in one cast.

Another factor that will influence your ability to shoot line is the profile of your line. In the chapter on fly lines, I explain the difference between the traditional double-taper line and the variety of specialist spey tapers that are on the market. If you are using a double taper, the thick belly has a lot of weight and drag as it goes through the rod rings, making it impossible to shoot great distances. The best spey casters could shoot no more than 20 to 25 feet of double taper in one go. However, with the thin running line of a short-head spey taper, it is possible to shoot a lot more line, up to 80 feet. Some of the best Scandinavians are masters with their shooting heads, and with this system, a really good caster could shoot 100 feet of line. It all boils down to simple physics. The thicker the fly line, the more the drag there is and the less the distance it will shoot.

If you are fishing a small river or a narrow pool, and don't need to shoot any line, you should aim the forward cast about 5 degrees above the horizontal. This will allow the line to unroll parallel to the water and fully turn over before landing on the water.

To shoot a relatively short length of line, you need to aim slightly higher.

To shoot a lot of line, the cast's trajectory should be substantially raised.

This cast has plenty of height and time for the loop to take as much line as is needed.

Shooting this much line with all the line washed downstream of you will result in a lot of drag and less shooting distance.

The last factor that affects the distance you can cast is the drag of line on the water. If you have 60 feet of line lying in the water, the drag from the surface tension can considerably hold back how far the line travels, particularly if the line is washed downstream in a great loop. If you can reduce the amount of line dragging on the water, you will increase your distance. There are a number of ways of doing this. First you can put your line in a strip-ping basket attached to your waist. This completely stops any drag of line through the water and the only real disadvantage is that a lot of line coiled in a basket can tangle! (There is also a problem when wading up to your waist!) Another solution is to lay the line on the water, but before casting, pull the line in and create four or five smaller loops attached to different fingers. This is okay and works very well, but can result in the odd tangle as you let go of four

This is exactly the same amount of line as the previous photo, but the caster is holding the middle of the large loop in the index finger of the bottom hand. These four small loops have a lot less drag on the line when it comes to shooting distance and rarely tangle.

loops of line at once. It also takes some practice, as you have to make sure you let go of all five fingers on the line at the same time. With anything but the very longest lines to shoot, I pull in about half of what is lying on the water and loop this around the index finger of my bottom hand. I've found this the most reliable method for getting the distance and for avoiding the tangles. I have also seen a very good spey caster who held a loop or two in his mouth!

This worked well for him but does not appeal to me (and I don't recommend it!) The final way, certain to avoid tangles though the least effective with distance, is to have only one coil (or two) hanging down in the river in a big loop. Try each way, dismiss what doesn't work or feel comfortable, and you will be left with your answer.

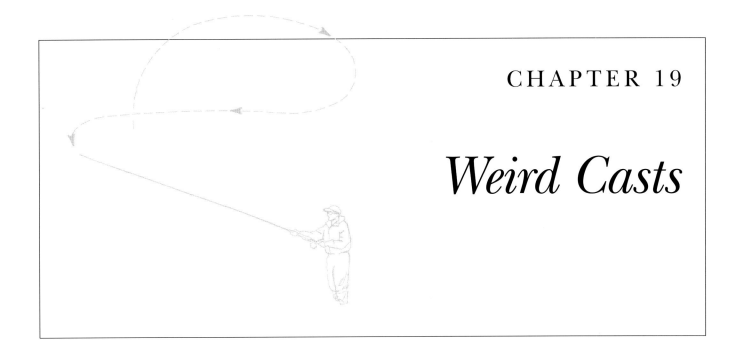

CHAPTER 19

Weird Casts

All types of cast have developed because of particular situations and the need to overcome problems. There will always be new casts appearing on the casting scene and new ones to master. Take the snake roll and the snap T—the two newest casts in this book. For years anglers got by with the double spey and single spey. The new casts do what these two classic casts do. They overcome the same situations and have no use that cannot be achieved with the traditional casts, so why learn them?

Partly because it's fun. Or perhaps we want to learn new casts to impress. "Wow, look at that caster over there—I have never seen anything like that before!" And partly it is to test ourselves. The more casts you are competent at, the more satisfying it is. You may only need the single and double spey to cope with any fishing situation (providing you can do them with both hands). But, when the fish aren't taking, casting is a great way of enjoying the day.

I have seen a lot of weird casts that have become established in various parts of the world and that all fall into the spey category. There is a reverse-snake-roll-pick-up-into-single-spey (called a spiral spey by some), a jump-release-into-single-spey, a behind-the-head-flick-into-snake-roll cast, the perry poke, the dry-fly spey, the oozlum spey, and Derek Brown's corkscrew cast (which he admits is useless for fishing, but is a wonderfully impressive cast and quite a skill to master). In addition to these, there are a number of unnameable movements and casts that have found their ways onto the waters of the world and can be considered part of the spey family.

SPIRAL SPEY

Some of these wonderful casts do find their way into fishing situations. The spiral spey is a nice way of breaking the surface tension and cleanly picking the line off the water before doing a single spey. Not only does it break the water surface cleanly, but it also enables you to position the anchor point easily and accurately. One of the best American spey casters I know, Steve Choate, uses this cast as his standard way of doing the single spey. He used it to great effect in 2002 at the spey casting competition held at the annual CLA game fair in England, winning the competition with a cast of fifty yards.

Though similar to the single spey, the great advantage this cast has is that the C shape makes the fly line break the surface film at the start of the cast very cleanly, making it much easier to position the anchor point. It's easier to place and a lot less work as you have all the line airborne when you start the backstroke; whereas with the single spey the line is still lying on the water and has to be broken free.

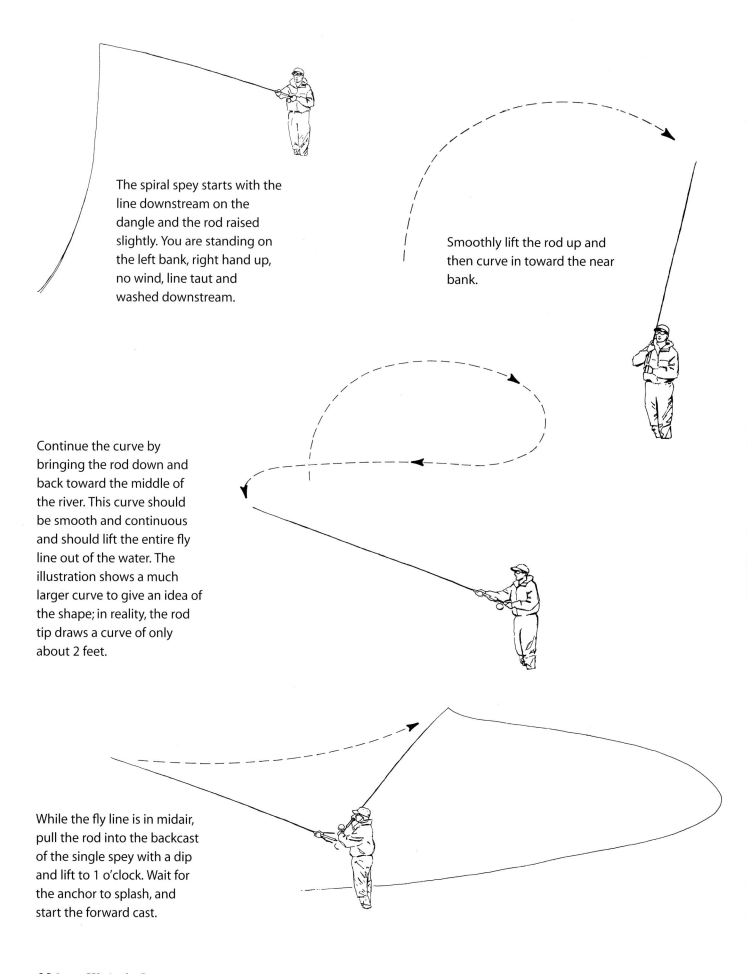

The spiral spey starts with the line downstream on the dangle and the rod raised slightly. You are standing on the left bank, right hand up, no wind, line taut and washed downstream.

Smoothly lift the rod up and then curve in toward the near bank.

Continue the curve by bringing the rod down and back toward the middle of the river. This curve should be smooth and continuous and should lift the entire fly line out of the water. The illustration shows a much larger curve to give an idea of the shape; in reality, the rod tip draws a curve of only about 2 feet.

While the fly line is in midair, pull the rod into the backcast of the single spey with a dip and lift to 1 o'clock. Wait for the anchor to splash, and start the forward cast.

The spiral spey starts with the line downstream on the dangle and the rod lifting up to about 11 o'clock, pointing slightly out into the river.

The rod tip draws a high but small **C** shape, lifting the fly line off the water and putting a distinctive wave in the line.

This **C** shape gets all the line airborne and makes it easy to start the backcast, which follows the same shape and path as the single spey.

Pull the rod tip behind and up to 1 o'clock and then wait
for the anchor to land.

Splash and go!

The perry poke is similar to the single spey or snap T—cast right hand up from the left bank with an upstream wind or no wind. The line starts washed downstream and tight. Lift the rod to about 11 o'clock, slightly angled out toward the river.

PERRY POKE

Another cast that has found its way into fishing use is the perry poke. A North American spey caster by the name of Ed Ward has started to popularize this cast in the United States. It is a useful way of energizing the line and is particularly suited to short belly spey lines and shooting heads. The cast may look a little weird when first seen, but the results that can be achieved by a master of this spey cast, like Ed, are astonishing. The perry poke is achieved by starting the cast like a single spey. On the left bank of a river in no wind, you start the cast with the line washed tight downstream and your right hand up. Lift the rod up smoothly to about 11 o'clock and swing the rod back around behind you to about 1 o'clock and opposite your target. There needs to be just enough

Swing the rod back upstream and around behind your body, similar to the single spey, but without the dip. The fly and all the fly line must land upstream of your target.

speed to lift the fly line out of the water on your downstream side and allow it to land in the water just upstream of your orange line. As soon as the fly lands on the water, do a halfhearted forward stroke toward your target and down that makes the line dump in front of you. Then finish off with a switch cast toward the target. The cast works very well because the dump on the initial forward cast means there is a large pile of slack on the water in front of you, and thus, when you throw the switch cast back, you have very little line drag to throw against and the belly flies behind you cleanly and easily. More importantly, the entire belly and line stick is 180 degrees from your target, giving maximum load to the rod—something that is quite tricky to master with the single spey.

Let the fly line land on the water and then gently dump the forward cast in front of you and slightly upstream of your target. Don't worry about all the slack on the water in front of you, as the next stage will get rid of that.

Kick the rod back low and flat to the side and then up
to 1 o'clock and opposite your target—just like a switch
cast.

Wait for the belly to tighten, and then drive against it on the forward cast. The strength of the perry poke is that the fly line is close to the caster and everything aligns in a perfect 180-degree plane. It is much more difficult for the beginner to get such energy in the backcast on a single spey.

A good result.

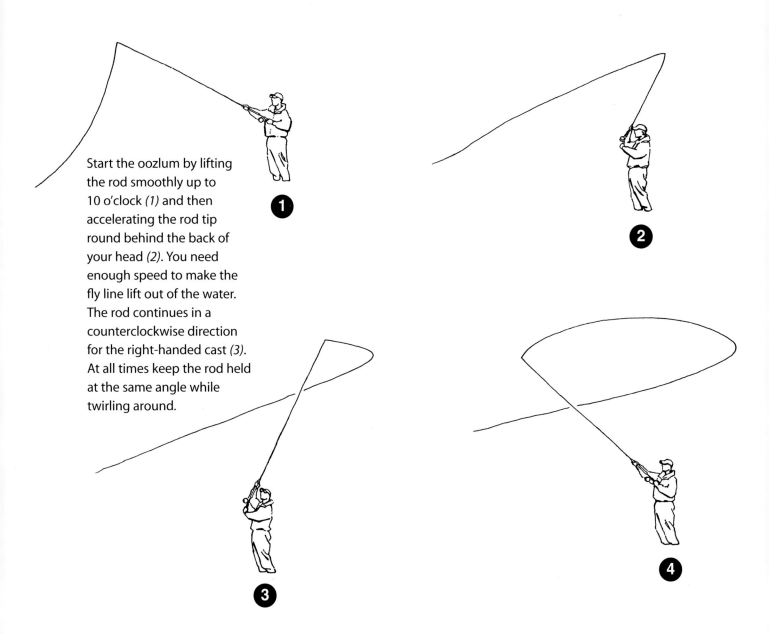

Start the oozlum by lifting the rod smoothly up to 10 o'clock *(1)* and then accelerating the rod tip round behind the back of your head *(2)*. You need enough speed to make the fly line lift out of the water. The rod continues in a counterclockwise direction for the right-handed cast *(3)*. At all times keep the rod held at the same angle while twirling around.

OOZLUM SPEY

Some other casts are completely useless for fishing. I mentioned Derek's corkscrew cast earlier as a good example. Another is the oozlum spey, which is a cast I have taught for many years just for fun. It is a good way of testing your ability in line control, but you would never use it to fish with. This cast is done by twirling your rod over your head in a big circle—just like a helicopter rotor—with enough speed to keep the fly line airborne. Then you duck the rod out of the circular path and into a single spey. I doubt any-one will be able to learn the cast from these few words and illustrations, but it falls into the category of fun—not fishing!

There are a number of casts that I have seen done by many good and average casters that have no names. They have been developed to solve a particu-lar problem. Some work and evolve into casts used by anglers, like the snake roll, the snap T, and the perry poke, and some will never be seen on a river-bank. The fun for the dedicated spey caster is in cre-ating and mastering such enjoyable casts.

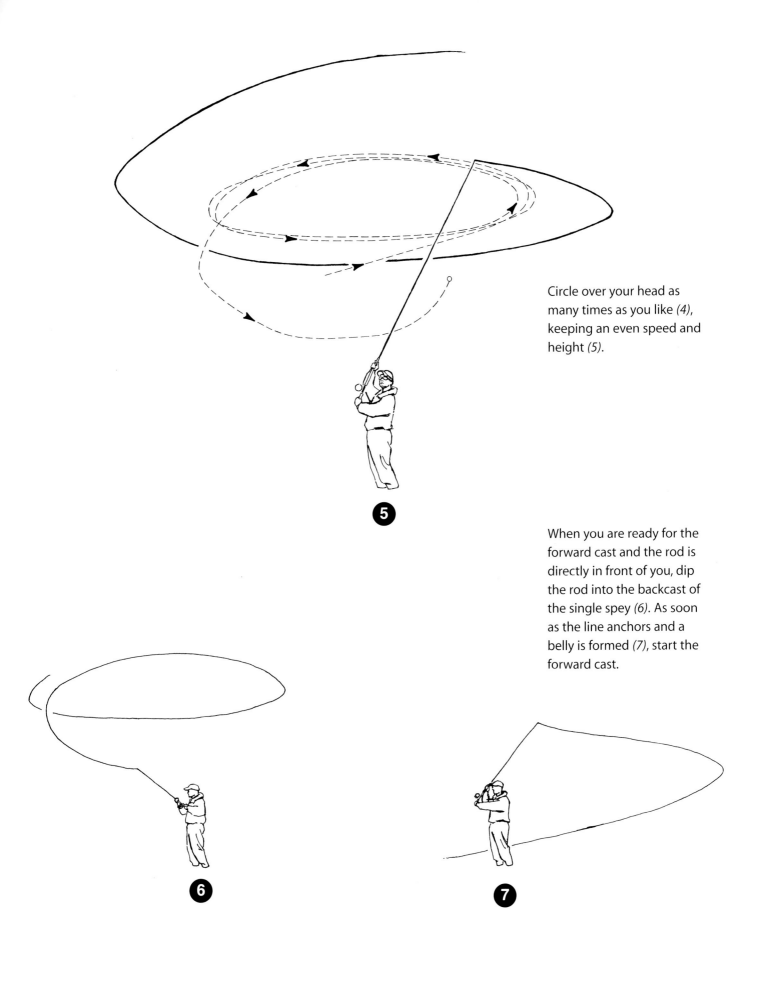

Circle over your head as many times as you like (4), keeping an even speed and height (5).

When you are ready for the forward cast and the rod is directly in front of you, dip the rod into the backcast of the single spey (6). As soon as the line anchors and a belly is formed (7), start the forward cast.

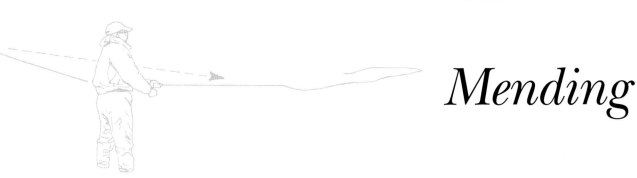

CHAPTER 20

Mending

There is more to successful fishing and catching fish than being able to cast out a good line. Another important skill is in controlling the way the fly fishes through the water. The extra length of two-handed rods helps with this. You can lift a much longer line off the water and, therefore, reposition the line to change the swing of the fly.

It is pointless to cast out a long line of 120 feet if the fly drags throughout its swing and is unappealing to the fish. A general rule of thumb is: "In slow water, speed the fly up. In fast water, slow the fly down." If you are fishing a pool on the river that is slow flowing, you need to utilize as much current as you can to keep the fly swinging and the fish interested. This is achieved by mending the line downstream. Conversely, in a swift current, the fly would likely sweep around too fast, so the object is to slow down its swing by reducing the pressure of the current on the line. Do this by mending the line upstream. With the lift you get from a 15- or 16-foot rod, you can reposition 90 to 100 feet of line easily with these long deadly casts.

You can do this most effectively with a double-taper or long belly spey line. Once you have cast out the thin running line of a spey taper, and particularly a shooting head, there is not enough weight to throw an effective mend. For fishing, the double taper wins every time.

The standard problem of a sinking line is that you cannot throw a mend into it. While this is true

Mending the line downstream speeds up the swing of the fly.

Mending the line upstream slows the swing of the fly.

For an aerial mend, you complete the forward stroke of a spey cast and move the rod smoothly and quickly upstream well before the line lands.

with an ordinary mend, when the angler attempts to reposition the line after it has landed and can't do so because it has sunk, it is not so with an aerial mend. This is a cast that most good trout anglers use, throwing a mend into the line in midcast so that the line lands and starts fishing correctly instantly. Why not with a spey cast—with a single or two-handed rod? The spey cast, or overhead cast, is completed in the

usual manner, though the forward cast trajectory is slightly higher. As you shoot line on the forward cast, move the rod tip in a flat side-to-side movement, though slow and steady. This has the effect of putting a large curve in the line—upstream or downstream, depending on which way the river flows and which way you moved the rod.

Before the line lands, bring the rod back downstream to point where you want the fly to land. When the fly line lands, the mend will already be in place.

A better option if you really want to be able to control your fly's swing and get depth is to use a sinking-tip line so that you have plenty of floating portion to lift and mend. This works particularly well and is how I would recommend going about fishing a deep fly, if you still want control of the mend. Just make sure that you have a tip long and dense enough to get the depth you want.

Once you have mastered some sort of mend with the sinking line, you will find the fly fishes a lot more effectively. You should not believe that the fly is not dragging just because your line has sunk and everything is under the water.

Fishing with a Two-Handed Rod

Although this is a book on spey casting, I do want to talk a bit about fishing techniques, not how you catch fish or which flies to use, but how the longer rods can help you control the way a fly fishes in the water. If you think the longer two-handed rods are great for casting, wait until you see how easily they help you control the fly in the water.

The fly's speed, depth, and the way it swings through a pool are the key factors that determine whether a fish will take the fly. These change with water height, temperature, and how fresh the fish are, and successful anglers are constantly thinking and changing their fishing techniques when times are tough and the fishing slow.

One simple way to remember the variables is to remember to keep "changing the MAT." MAT is the acronym I use for mend, angle, tension—the three factors that control how the line swings across the current.

MEND

Since I talked about mending in the previous chapter, I won't repeat that information again here. I find many anglers use the mend too often and, unfortunately, without thought. It is no good mending every cast and having it swing through the pool the same way it did on as the last cast. Sometimes

you need to mend, but there are plenty of times when you don't need a mend and all a mend will do is slow the fly down (or speed it up) unnecessarily. I often see anglers mending in situations that don't need a mend, and they catch fewer fish because they are putting in a mend. There are two other factors that are just as important as the mend in getting the fly's swing right.

ANGLE

The angle you cast the line to the current is another way of controlling the speed the fly swings through the pool. The more square the line is cast, the more direct push the current has on the line and the faster it will swing. Conversely, the tighter the angle the line is cast to the current, the weaker the current will push against it and the slower the line will swing. In fast water currents, you tend to want a slower swing. This is accomplished by casting the line at a tight angle to the current (and possibly mending). As you move down the river, you will come across slower pools that need a cast that is squarer to the current so that the line does swing and gives the fly some life. In really slow pools, you'll need to make a square cast at 90 degrees with a downstream mend and strip the line to give the fly enticing movement and attract the attention of something out there.

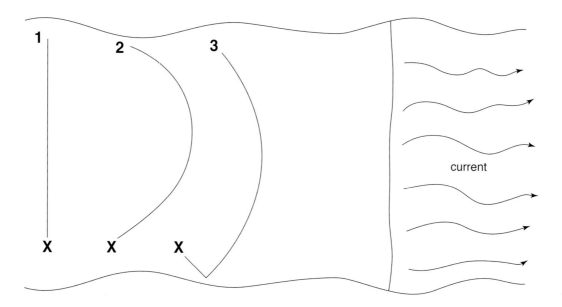

When fishing a slow pool, like this one above a weir, you need to give the fly movement to attract the fish's attention. This is best achieved by first casting square to the current (1), throwing a downstream mend into the line (2), and moving the rod toward your own bank to increase the drag on the line (3). Additional speed can be imparted to the fly, if necessary, by stripping the fly.

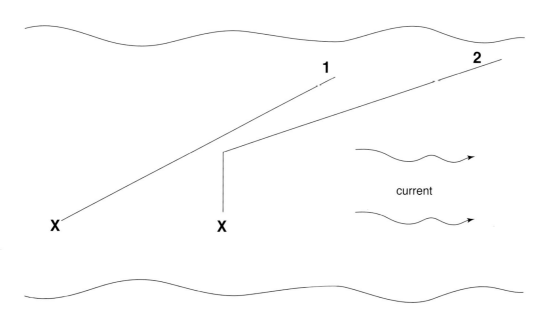

In faster current, make a cast at a much tighter angle so there is less direct pressure on the line from the current, giving the line a slower swing (1). By pushing the rod tip out into the current, you will get an even tighter angle of line to the current and a slower swing (2). As the line swings around the current, let the line lead the rod around for an even slower swing. Finally, if necessary, add an upstream mend to get a slower and more controlled swing.

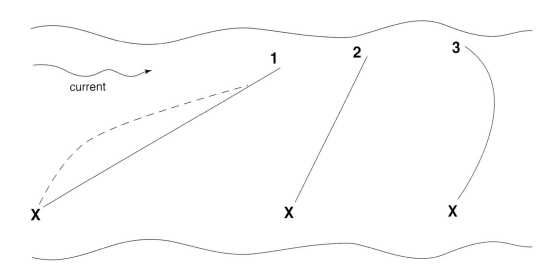

When working through a pool, the successful angler varies the angle of the cast as the water speed changes. At the head of the pool, a tight angle cast with an upstream mend is usually most productive *(1)*. As you work down the pool and come to slower water, the casts should get a little squarer *(2)*. In the slowest part of the pool, a square cast with a downstream mend is necessary to keep the fly interesting to the fish *(3)*.

TENSION

The tension of the line as it swings around in the current controls the depth the fly fishes. When there is no tension, the line and fly will drift downstream at the same rate as the current and sink. As soon as the line tightens, the fly line will start to swing across the current and lift the fly toward the surface. The amount of lift depends on the speed of the current and the tension in the line. The faster the current and the tighter the line, the more the lift, assuming you're using a floating line. One of the most deadly fishing techniques I know is called controlled drag, and its controlling factor is the tension of the line. The diagram below helps explain the way the fishing

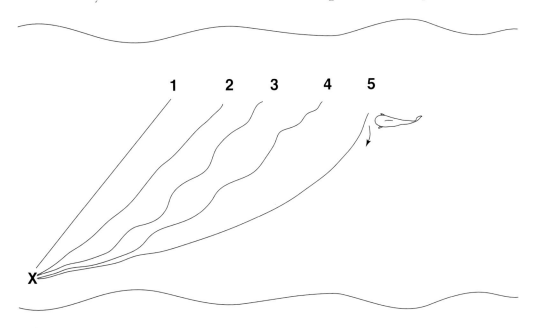

Controlled drag is one of the most effective fishing techniques if you know where a fish is lying. Start by casting well upstream of the fish and slightly farther across from the fish *(1)*. Immediately, as the line lands, start paying out slack, just faster than the current *(2 and 3)*. When you have enough slack out, stop paying the line and hold the line tight *(4)*. The line will tighten, and the fly will dart across the fish's nose, making an irresistible target *(5)*.

technique works. Controlled drag is effective when you know where the fish is or if you are fishing controlled drag to the most likely lies in the river. You start by casting the line directly upstream of the fish, say 10 to 12 feet and slightly beyond the fish. As soon as the line lands, you need to pay out slack faster than the current and judge the amount of slack so that it runs out just as the fly reaches the fish. The line will become tight, and the fly will suddenly lift in front of the fish and start to sweep across its nose. How infuriating this is to a fish! The fish has had a long view of a fly drifting in the current toward it, seemingly unaware, then this little grunt jumps in front of the fish and has the temerity to dart away! The fish's natural instinct is to lunge after the annoying interloper and bite it, which is just what the angler wants!

Tension is also a good way to get extra depth when the current is strong or the water cold. There are situations where I have cast my line *upstream* at an angle of 45 degrees so the line drifts downstream slack in the current and sinking until it is tight when it will swing around. When doing this, you need to keep mending so that the line, when it starts to swing, is in full control, and it will give you extra depth if you haven't got a fast-enough sinking tip or a heavy-enough fly with you.

Controlled drag is deadly effective and has worked for me all over the world for salmon, steelhead, and trout. I even tried it on an eel once and caught it! As a successful angler, you need to be constantly changing your fishing technique as you work your way down a pool, and the easiest way to do this is to keep changing your MAT.

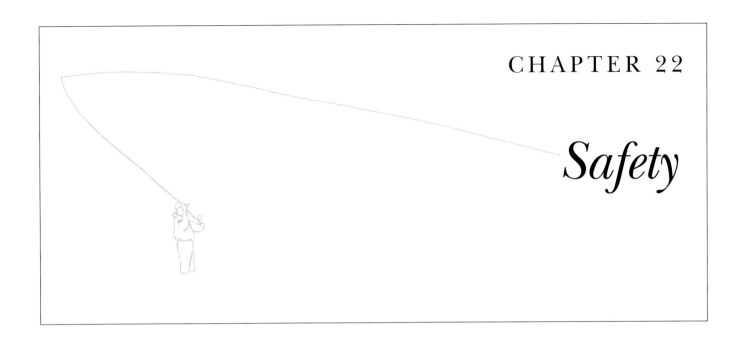

CHAPTER 22

Safety

When you first arrive at the river, check the direction of the wind and use the right cast for the conditions. Be aware of the wind at all times, and when it changes direction, change your cast.

Always wear eye protection and a hat.

Wade within your limits. Remember, two-handed rods cast much farther than single-handed rods, so there should be no reason for you to wade too deep. Make sure you have a firm stance before making a cast. Take a wading staff if going into deep or strong water, and where possible, wade with the current, not against it.

Make sure you tape your rod joints with a suitable tape. Electrical tape works well and comes off easily, without leaving too much sticky residue. Taping is important. Spey casting generates a lot of torque and twist on a rod and most rod joints slide apart during a couple hours of casting. If you are lucky, you can catch this before the rod flies apart. If you are unlucky, one rod section will slide almost all

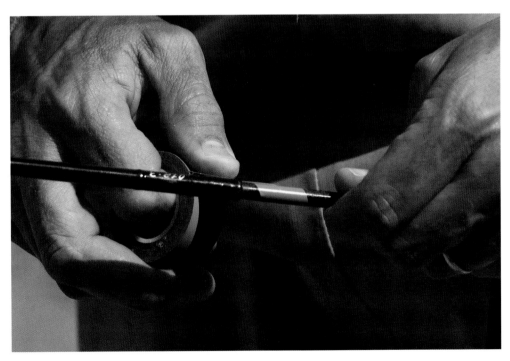

Always tape your rod sections before you start spey casting to keep the rod from coming apart or even breaking.

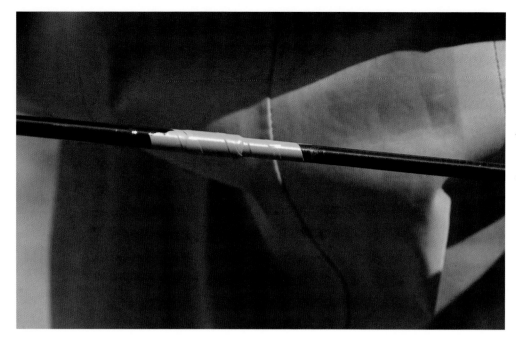

The finished taping should be neat so that a loose end doesn't catch the line.

the way out, leaving not enough support in the ferrule for the power of the cast and the rod will snap at the ferrule. I have seen this happen too many times.

When you are standing close to or on the riverbank, look above, around, and behind you for overhanging trees so you can avoid hitting one with your rod and breaking the tip off.

If you have any distance to walk from the car to the pool you are going to fish, avoid rigging your rod up at the car. You may have to walk through trees and bushes and carrying a disassembled rod through obstacles is a lot easier than carrying a rod already made up.

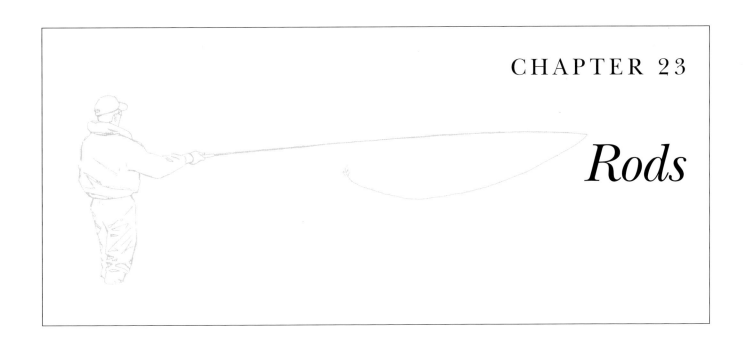

CHAPTER 23

Rods

Easy spey casting comes down to two factors— ability and tackle. You can improve if you get good instruction and practice.

And you can choose the right tackle. What works for one caster will not necessarily work for another. Like the single-handed rods, there are dozens and dozens of different types of two-handed rods on the market. They vary in length, line rating, action, and weight, and without doubt, the best thing to do is try out a few rods to find one that suits your casting style and budget.

A selection of two-handed rods. From the top: a Scott SAS (now called the A2), a Loomis GLX, a Sage 5120, and a Thomas and Thomas DH 1409. With the exception of the Sage rod, which is a #5 trout spey rod, all of these rods are very light and fast, and they are among my favorite rods to cast.

LENGTH

The length of the rod you choose depends on how far you want to cast—i.e., how wide the river is. The shortest proper two-handed rod on the market (at the time of this writing) is 10 feet long and made by Thomas & Thomas, while the longest is made by Daiwa at 18 feet. Here are some rough guidelines (subject to line weight) for the length of rod I would choose for the size of river (or distance) I would want to fish comfortably.

Rod Length (in feet)	Distance Cast (in feet)
11	90
12	105
13	115
14	125
15	140
16	150
17	160
18	170

These are all pretty big casts for the rod length and only achievable by spey casters with excellent technique. Perhaps a more realistic chart for the average spey caster would be this.

Rod Length (in feet)	Distance Cast (in feet)
11	65
12	75
13	85
14	90
15	100
16	105
17	105
18	105

It is quite a skill to manage the longer rod lengths, and this is why I don't believe that the average caster would be able to get any farther with an 18-foot rod than with a 16-foot rod.

In his book *Fine and Far Off*, Jock Scott gives a table for greenheart rods.

Rod Length (in feet)	Distance Cast
13	32 yards (96 feet)
14	35 yards (105 feet)
15	38 yards (114 feet)
16	41 yards (123 feet)
17	44 yards (132 feet)
18	47 yards (141 feet)
19	50 yards (150 feet)
20	53 yards (159 feet)

Jock's distances "represented the lengths of line which can *comfortably be picked up and thrown, without shooting.*" I feel the distances quoted by Jock Scott to be exaggerated and think these figures are impossible to reach without shooting line.

These lists are ambiguous, anyway, as they don't take into account the line weight, the type of line, wind, fly size and weight, rod action, wading depth, and whether the line is a floater, a sink tip, or a sinker. Just take wading depth, for a moment. For every foot deeper you wade, you lose at least 10 feet in the distance you cast. This follows the rod length guide a little, as a 14-foot rod casts 10 feet less than a 15-foot rod. You may lose even more when you get to the depths that involve holding your hands higher above your head to avoid dunking your elbows in the river. With this kind of wading, I would say you are more likely to lose 15 feet per rod/foot length than 10.

The longer the rod, the better control you will have of the fly as it fishes through the water. It is much easier to mend the line at long distance with a longer rod than with a short rod. The longer rods have more lift to them, which makes it easier to lift a full sinking line, or deep sunk tip to the surface, or

Wading deep drastically reduces the distance you can cast.

roll cast it, in order to cast out again. But landing a fish on your own is tougher with a long rod. This presents no problem if you are fishing near a gravel beach on which you can beach the fish, or a companion or ghillie can net or hand tail the fish for you. But sometimes you hook a decent fish when you're wading fairly deep on your own with nothing but high banks and trees behind you. In this situation it is devilishly tough to land the fish without leading the fish out of the pool. A shorter rod does make it more possible to bring the fish closer to you and somehow grab or net on your own.

There are a number of factors to take into account when you're purchasing a two-handed rod, and the lists comparing rod length to casting distance are guidelines to help you make a good selection.

If you fish a medium-size river, with relatively small fish (4 to 5 pounds) and low summer conditions, don't buy a 15-foot rod just so you can get the maximum distance. Remember the fun of the fight. A 15-foot rod is too heavy to get a good fight from a worthwhile quarry, and a shorter rod, for a lighter line, is a better choice.

LINE RATING

Two-handed salmon rods are designed to cast heavier lines than trout rods and, traditionally, are rated for lines between 8 and 12 weight. Line weights tend to follow rod lengths. Usually, the longer rods are built for the heavier lines—a 14-foot rod for a 9- or a 10-weight line, a 15-foot rod for a 10- or 11-weight line and so on, though this is changing and many manufacturers have longer rods with light line ratings. At the time of this writing, for example, Sage has a 12-foot rod rated for a 5-weight line—designed for the trout fly fisher—and a 14-foot rod for a 7-weight line. Thomas & Thomas has a 10-foot rod for a 6-weight line and a 13-foot rod for a 7-weight line. These rods are great performers and break from the mold of longer rods and heavier lines.

The factors that influence your choice of rod by line rating is how far you want to cast, how deep you want to fish (or how powerful the current is flowing), and how big the fish are that you are (hopefully!) going to catch.

The heavier the line, the farther you can cast it. If you are looking for a rod to cast maximum distance, you should consider something at least 15

At the time of this writing, Sage's 5120 was the lightest two-handed rod on the market and an absolute joy to use for trout, grilse, sea trout, and smaller summer-run steelhead.

feet or 16 feet and rated for a 10- or 11-weight line. A good caster with a 15-foot rod may be able to cast 140 feet. Since you can get a 15-foot rod rated for anything from a 7- to a 12-weight line, length isn't the only consideration for distance. The line rating must also be taken into account. The difference in distance between a 15-foot 7-weight rod and a 15-foot 11-weight rod can be as much as 50 feet.

There's another reason for looking at the AFTMA rod ratings. If you are going to be fishing heavy sinking lines, or big heavy tube, or lead-eyed flies, the heavier line-rated rods will handle the really fast sinking tips and sinking lines a lot better than their lighter cousins will. And the heavier fly lines will cast the heaviest flies easier. To choose a rod to fish the Tweed in late October, you have to consider that you will need a deep sunk line and a large, heavy tube fly. For this type of fishing, you need to look at a rod with at least an 11-weight rating, if not a 12. You may not need to cast it far, but the weight of the fly and depth that the line will be means that you need these heavier rods.

In the United States, where sinking tips are much more popular than full sinking lines, you can fish deeper by adding various lengths (and sinking rates) of tips to the floating line. The weight of the main body of the line must be heavy enough to carry the

weight of the sink tip. It is easy enough if using the standard 15-foot tips that are supplied with the many interchangeable tip lines. These tips usually weigh the same for a given AFTMA number—for example the 15-foot 10-weight tips I use all weigh 150 grains. They vary considerably in *density*, which truly effects how fast these tips sink. In my 10-weight tips wallet I have an intermediate tip that sinks about 2 inches per second, a type 3 tip (3 inches per second), a type 6 tip (6 inches per second), and a type 8 tip (8 inches per second), but they all weigh 150 grains. This makes sense because it means that whatever tip I choose I know the grain weight of the line isn't going to change and I don't have to adjust my casting technique. However, with the longer sinking tips, their weights change with their sinking speeds. The popular weights of the longer sink tips, like the 24-foot Big Boy tips from RIO, are 150, 200, 300, 400, and 500 grains. You need at least a 10-weight floating line body to carry the 500-grain tip, a 9-weight body for the 400-grain tip, and so on down the scale. So, if you need to get deep and have to buy one of these longer, heavier sink tips, you will need to keep that in mind when choosing the rod's AFTMA rating.

The final consideration when choosing a rod based on its AFTMA rating is the size of the fish you are after and how sporting you want to be. A perfect rod for summer run grilse or summer run steelhead in the Californian rivers is going to be a light 7 or 8 weight. For trout fishing, why choose anything heavier than a 5- or 6-weight rod? These rods will cast smaller flies easily and feel so much more fun than a great big 10 weight if you're fishing for small fish in low water.

ACTION

Spey rods are available in two types of actions. Both have their followers and anyone taking up spey casting or wishing to improve needs to find the action they get on best with. The spey casts will differ one action to the other. Here is a guideline of each type and its advantages.

Fast/Modern/Tip Action

Back in the early '90s when I was teaching spey casting on my home river in Devon, a client booked a two-day spey casting course and brought with him his new acquisition, a 15-foot 10-weight Sage spey rod from America. It was fast and tippy and nothing like any I had ever come across before. It changed my life. This rod could cast such a long line and was so light and controllable that I immediately fell in love with it. I couldn't believe that a nation with no spey casting history could produce a rod so vastly superior to anything on the market in that day in the United Kingdom. That was it; from then on I was hooked on light, fast-action salmon rods.

The advantage of the faster action is that the rod reacts instantly to your every movement. Like the single-handed rod, these fast two-handed rods can throw nice, tight loops on the forward cast, reducing air resistance and getting extra distance. Faster action rods also make it a lot easier to cast that dream loop: the one that every spey caster has seen photos of and wants to be able to do—the one that unrolls perfectly in the air, traveling horizontally as it goes out, not rolling along the water like a large barrel of lard. As a result of these wonderful loops, you can cast out a line with little effort—or you should be able to! Because the loops are so much smaller and cut through the air better than the loops from a traditional-action salmon/spey rod, you can achieve greater distance. These faster action rods also pick up deep sunk tips and lines much easier than their slower counterparts and cast much better on a windy day. They also feel so good!

All in all, the faster action rods have many advantages, and the only down side is that they are not forgiving. You need to be a reasonably good caster to get the best from these rods and you also should favor a style of casting that leans toward the modern style rather than the traditional style. (See "The Crude Spey" chapter for the differences.) You'll need to be able to emphasize the work of your lower hand on the rod and make the short, positive stop required to get these rods working so well. With these faster rods, give a short, sharp tug with the bottom hand in conjunction with a wrist snap of the upper arm for a perfect power stroke to make the most of the rod's potential. You'll get those wonderful loops. For casters who consistently cannot get the bottom hand to do any work, I suggest using a more traditional-action rod.

Traditional/Through Action

This action has been around since the first spey rods were made. The rod bends through most of the blank (even way into the cork handle on some I have tried!) and needs little effort to get loaded. This action is not my favorite. For me, these rods are too slow and don't cast long distances or beat strong upstream winds. Where they are useful is for casters who use no power. The softness of the rod has a natural sway to it that can cast the line out of its own accord. Though this isn't for me, I have found it a helpful tool in my classes, as occasionally I come across casters who haven't the feel for spey casting. With this softer action, they pick up the feel.

With the softer action rods, there is no snap in the forward cast—just smoothness. If you snap, you will certainly get a tailing loop. And the wide grip isn't so important. You can cast these rods quite effectively with your two hands only inches from either side of the reel, providing that the balance is perfect. (See the chapter on reels.)

In days gone by, sadly, there were no British companies that made the faster action rods. They all produced the traditional actions. Sage started it for me, then Loomis, then Thomas & Thomas—American companies that made light, fast spey rods. I used to quiver with anticipation when I got a Loomis GLX 15-foot 10-weight rod in my hand, or the

Thomas & Thomas DH 15-foot 11-weight rod, or the DH 14-foot 9-weight. Nowadays Hardy, Daiwa, and Bruce & Walker from the United Kingdom and Burkheimer, Orvis, Redington, St. Croix, Scott, and Winston from the United States make wonderful spey rods.

A word on multipiece rods. I am sure that one day someone will come up with a 7-piece two-handed rod. The advances in rod technology have meant that multipiece rods are no longer extra heavy and extra soft and the popularity of these in the single-handed rods has soared. This is starting to happen in the spey world. The first multipiece I owned was made by Thomas & Thomas. I was consulting for them at the time and suggested it would be a good idea to have travel friendly spey rods. Tom Dorsey, the rod designer and brains behind Thomas & Thomas, produced a 15-foot 10-weight 5-piece rod. They already made a superb 15-foot 10-weight 3-piece rod, and I remember trying out these two rods side by side on the river behind the T & T factory. The 5-piece rod was as good as the 3-piece in every way and better in that it could be transported more easily. I am still in awe of Tom's ability to create such terrific rods. Winston collaborated with the great Scottish spey caster, Derek Brown, to produce a series of 15-foot 5-piece rods. And I am sure there are—and will be—others. The only challenge with these multipiece rods is that it takes time to tape the ferrules!

WEIGHT

In the old days, a heavy rod was desirable because it was believed the heavier weight helped to get the line out, through inertia, I guess. Now, modern technology and carbon fibers have brought the overall weight of a two-handed rod down from several pounds to less than 10 ounces. These lighter rods require less effort to cast and are more pleasurable to fish with—particularly when you have on a small summer-run grilse.

I remember once trying a Hardy 18-foot double built steel-shafted Palakona rod (split cane, of course). I don't know how old this weapon was as a client had brought it down for a spey casting lesson. It weighed 54 ounces—3 pounds, 6 ounces! What a beast of burden. I was tired in minutes, though it put out a nice line. Men had muscles in the old days! While we're on the subject, if you have a heavy fly rod, don't be fooled into putting on a lightweight reel to try and keep down the overall weight. If you put a lovely light modern spey reel on a fairly heavy rod, the balance point is so far up the rod and away from the cork grip that it's difficult to cast. A heavier reel will make things easier. For more about this, see the chapter on reels.

In summary, when looking to buy a salmon/spey rod, first decide on the length you need, then on the line rating and action. If possible, try out one or two different rods of the type you've chosen and find the one you are comfortable with.

Here are some guidelines: Large rivers—15 or 16 feet for a 10- or 11-weight line. Medium rivers or one all-round rod—14 feet for a 9-weight line. Small rivers—12 to 13 feet for a 7- or 8-weight line. As spey casting gets more popular, we are starting to see shorter and lighter rods designed for the trout fly fisher. I have used a 10-foot 5-weight full two-handed rod. It was incredible and just perfect for trout fishing wider rivers where you need a little more distance than the trees behind allow. I wonder what kinds of spey rods we'll see in the future, and I am looking forward to finding out.

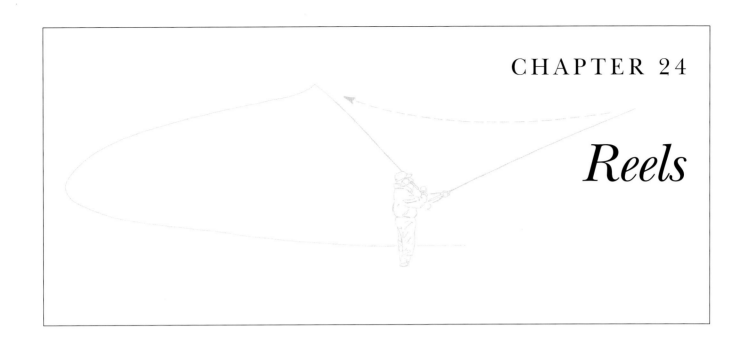

CHAPTER 24

Reels

There is little to say about reels in a book on casting. To help you avoid buying a reel that isn't going to be any good, here are the main things to look for.

WEIGHT

One of the simplest ways of reducing the amount of work you'll have to do to cast is to make sure that the whole outfit—the rod, reel, and line—you are using is balanced. Pay attention to the weight of the reel you put on the rod. A heavy 15-foot rod is completely out of balance with a light reel. On more than one occasion, I have seen someone with a heavy rod try to keep the weight of the outfit down by buying a lightweight reel. Don't do it. Ideally, the center of gravity, the balance point, should be where your upper hand holds the rod—with your fly line threaded up the rod and stripped out enough to cast. To test this, balance the rod on a finger. If it balances where you would hold it, the outfit is set up perfectly. If, as in many cases, the rod balances a foot up the blank, the reel is too light and you will have a lot more work to do—not to mention the extra strain that will be placed on your forearm tendons. If you are testing a rod in this way, make sure the rod is threaded up and you have a comfortable casting length of line outside the rod tip. An empty reel, or a reel with all the line wound in, will have a completely different balance point.

With the right reel choice, the rod should balance where your top hand holds the rod—with the line threaded up the rod and enough line out to cast.

Too light a reel or too heavy a rod and the point of balance is too far up the rod, making it very tiring work to cast.

A large arbor reel like this one from Waterworks makes the fly line less prone to develop annoying coils from being stored too tightly.

One of my many acquisitions over the years is a brass reel made by Daiwa. The whole thing weighs about 12 ounces and looks much too heavy to use. However, it balances my old, heavy 15- and 16-foot rods perfectly and really makes light work of using these big rods.

In this era of wanting everything as light as possible, reels, too, have gotten lighter. Testing a series of spey reels recently, I met with the designer on the Snake River in Idaho to give the reels a try. They were excellent: smooth, with a great drag system, beautiful to look at, and with the right amount of capacity needed for the modern spey lines. But they were too light. They were out of balance with the rods I used. The center of gravity was a good foot above the cork handle. The designer increased the weight of the reel and the new series of reels are lovely for spey casting and balance the average spey rods perfectly. Sometimes getting things lighter isn't always the right way to go.

CAPACITY

The other thing to be aware of when you're choosing a reel for spey casting is that it has to have enough capacity to hold plenty of backing (about 150 to 200 yards of 30-pound backing) and line. Modern spey lines are very long—up to 150 feet—and can have big, thick, heavy (and long) heads. You need a reel with a lot more capacity than you need with a trout line or a saltwater line. I know reel capacities differ from one manufacturer to the next, but as a guideline I have found that a size 12 reel will hold only a 9-weight spey line with sufficient backing. If you have a 11/12-weight spey line you have to get a bigger reel or have less backing. If in doubt, check the recommended capacity with the tackle shop before you buy.

ARBOR

Finally, for your convenience more than to help your casting, look for a reel with a large arbor. With a large arbor, you can speed up the winding in of the fly line at the end of the day or when you move from pool to pool. More importantly, it stores the fly line on the reel in much larger coils, thus giving your fly line a longer life and avoiding those annoying coils that can tangle up as you are shooting line on the forward cast.

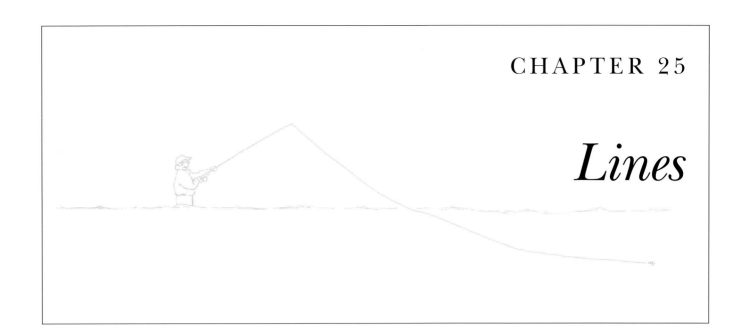

CHAPTER 25

Lines

Your choice of fly line can seriously affect your cast and influence what style of spey caster you become. Fly lines are continually being designed and redesigned, changing and evolving, and new line designs are introduced all the time. The aim in this chapter is not to tell you which line is right for you, but to let you know what line designs are available and when to use them. Then you can choose.

Fly lines differ in three main ways: weight, profile, and density.

WEIGHT

It used to be simple. Fly lines were designated with a number between 1 and 12 that related to the weight of the first 30 feet of line. Lines used to carry a single number. Lines for salmon fishing usually started as light as 8 and went up to a heavy 12. The bigger the number, the heavier the line and the stiffer the rod needed to handle it. These days spey casting fly lines are being assigned more numbers, and you will frequently see lines with three numbers, such as 9/10/11. This is kind of confusing but might make sense once explained. If the line has three numbers, it usually means that it is suitable for a rod of the middle number. In this example, a 9/10/11 line is best for a 10-weight rod. Jim Vincent of RIO products started the multinumber line system. He and a bunch of steelhead cronies were unhappy with the way a 10-weight line loaded a 10-weight rod, and after all, the system was originally designed for 30-

foot casts with single-handed rods, not 60-foot casts with two-handed rods. These steelhead guys used to cut up fly lines and splice them together to make customized lines which performed better than the regular 10 weights. Jim would splice together part of the front taper of a 10-weight line to the body of an 11-weight line and add to the front of that the taper of a 9-weight line. He then had a line with a much longer front taper than standard double-taper lines, and a line with plenty of energy and mass behind the taper to make casting big flies easy. Hence the three number designation. The finished 10-weight line had a lot more weight to it than a standard 10 weight and would load the two-handed spey rods a

Modern spey lines often have a three-number designation, and usually the middle number determines which rod it is designed for.

269

lot better. When Jim began to manufacture fly lines, he used this prototype to produce his specialist spey lines. At about the same time, in the United Kingdom Michael Evans was finding the same problems with the lines he used for salmon fishing and, as early as 1992, Michael started to produce his own specialty spey tapers and lines. According to Michael, "These tapers took into account important changes to the double-taper system. Extending the front taper made better use of the diminishing energy running through the heavier belly [and] the tapers threw out the real AFTMA weighing system, as it is/was wholly inappropriate for spey casting belly lengths." Michael, I believe, was also the first person to incorporate two colors in a spey line to easily distinguish where the rod should load.

I have seen students turn up for their lessons with 9-weight spey rods rigged with regular 9-weight forward lines. Although this sounds right, it isn't. Spey lines are so much heavier and longer in the head than regular weight forward lines that a regular 9-weight forward line will not come close to loading the rod. I use a WindCutter 8/9/10 on my 14-foot 9-weight rod, and it is a perfect balance. The head weight of the WindCutter (at 54 feet) is 585 grains. The AFTMA standard for a regular 9-weight forward line is 240 grains at 30 feet, with a head length of between 35 and 45 feet. For a two-handed salmon or spey rod, you want the extra head weight.

PROFILE

For many years the line choice for two-handed spey casters was limited to the double taper. For stability, versatility, and head length, it was hard to beat. Weight forward lines are useless for spey casting. Casts with big salmon rods are so long that there is a significant part of the running line outside the rod, lying on the water. Since it is impossible to spey cast with running line outside the rod guides, the double taper was the only choice. Many British casters still favor the double taper, and it certainly has its advantages—as we'll learn later.

Developments in tackle, plus a growing interest in spey casting have resulted in specialist spey casting lines becoming available. New taper designs have changed the world of spey casting. In the United States, Jim Vincent introduced special spey tapers, and in the United Kingdom, Michael Evans started designing his successful Arrowhead Twin-line

spey lines. Both fly-line designers came up with new fly-line profiles that were the heavier head, weight-forward type of lines for the big rods that were starting to become popular.

In the past, while the double taper had made it possible to load and use two-handed rods, beginners found them hard to use to get the distance they needed in bigger rivers. The modern spey lines are basically weight forwards, with heavy heads, long front tapers, and fairly short back taper tapering to the running line. A standard single-handed weight-forward line has a head between 35 and 45 feet, whereas modern spey lines have heads anywhere from 54 to 120 feet. These long heads are necessary to load spey rods for true spey casts.

The spey line with the shortest head available (at the time of this writing) is the Rio WindCutter. At 50 to 54 feet (apart from shooting heads), this line has proved so effective and easy to spey cast that other line manufacturers—Hardy, Airflo, S. A., and Cortland—have brought out their own versions. The WindCutter is without doubt the easiest line to learn to spey cast. For the steelhead fly fisher, it is also the easiest of the interchangeable tip-type lines to use for picking up deep sunken tips. I recommend this line for four kinds of fishing. For the beginning spey caster, there is no better line to learn with. For fishing the long, faster sinking heads (24 feet and longer), this is the easiest line to use to lift the deep sunk tips to the surface and cast them again. It's a great choice for shorter spey rods between 10 and 12 feet. Finally, for any spey caster who likes to get his distance by shooting the line, this line (or a Scandinavian-style shooting head) is the way to go.

Now let's look at the long-head spey lines. Scientific Anglers introduced the XLT (with a head length up to 120 feet) and RIO the GrandSpey (with a head up to 100 feet). These lines serve the needs of two types of casters: the true experts who want the best line for distance casting and who have the skill to handle these long head lengths and use them as long weight forwards, and the average spey casters who don't want yards of running line in the water to strip in and shoot out with each cast. These long lines are perfect for the cast-and-swing style of spey casting. Better than the original double taper lines, their front taper turns over flies much more effectively at long distances. The very long front tapers on these lines funnel the energy to the fly more

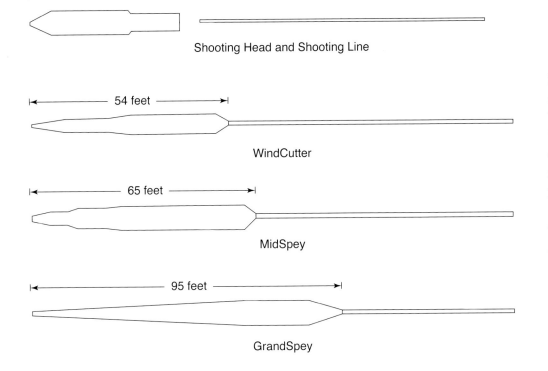

44 feet

Shooting Head and Shooting Line

54 feet

WindCutter

65 feet

MidSpey

95 feet

GrandSpey

Different head lengths of RIO's modern spey lines. The shorter the head length the easier it is to get distance, but the more stripping in between casts you have and the more problems managing all the loose line. *Thanks to RIO Products Intl., Inc.*

effectively than the mere 8- or 10-foot-long front tapers of most double taper lines.

The XLT and GrandSpey lines are based on a tried and tested design dating back to the 1800s. A Scotsman, Alexander Grant, was reputed to have cast 56 yards with a continuous-taper square-plait line. Two of America's finest spey casters, Steve Choate and Way Yin, used Grant's concept to design the XLT. The year that Steve and Way designed the XLT, Steve won the prestigious U.K. spey casting competition at the Game Fair with the XLT and a spey cast of 150 feet.

Designing the GrandSpey was an interesting project for me. Jim Vincent gave me the task of designing this line, and he kept me on the straight and narrow, making prototype after prototype, casting each one into the wind with big flies, sinking tips, and all kinds of spey rods. Finally we were satisfied. The line turned over heavy tips and big flies into a wind, yet cast easily with good presentation. It's a joy to cast.

Neither of these lines is for everyone. But for the spey caster who doesn't want to strip in line and have to shoot it out again, these are fine choices.

A more practical line for the good spey caster is the middle-head-length spey line—lines like the MidSpey, Airflo long Delta, or Wulff triangle taper. These are quite a bit longer than the short-head spey lines and nicer to cast once you become skilled with the spey rod. The longer head gives the line more stability in the air and doesn't require as much stripping as the WindCutter type line. It is still short enough for a caster with ability to shoot line and get extra distance easily, and the longer head makes it a better line to mend and fish the fly effectively.

The tapers of the various spey lines differ for other reasons, apart from how they shoot. The line manufacturers—RIO, Orvis, Scientific Anglers, Wulff, Loop, Hardy, Monic, Airflo, Cortland, and others—will tell you the pros and cons of their various designs. You'll have to sample them to find the line length and weight that loads your rod and works well for you.

DENSITY

The all-round fly fisher will find plenty of times when the fly has to get down deep, such as fishing in cold water conditions or deep pools, or strong currents, or high water conditions that push the fly too near the surface. Using a heavy fly like a brass tube fly or a lead dumbbell-head streamer is one way to get the fly down. Tying on a sinking leader is another. But

When using a sinking line or a sinking tip, you must get the line up to the surface before any of the spey casts can begin. One way to do this is to put enough lift at the start of the spey cast to lift about half the sink tip out of the water.

the best and most consistent way of controlling the depth of the fly is to use sinking lines or sink tips. Though they have a reputation for being tricky to cast, they are nowhere near as difficult as trying to pick up a heavy, deep-sunk 3-inch brass tube fly, and certainly they are easier to control.

In order to spey cast easily, the line and leader must be on or near the surface before you start the cast. It is no use trying to spey cast a sunk line without getting it up to the surface first. There are three ways to do this, depending on the type of line you use and how deep it is. If you are using a sink tip line and a short-headed line, like the WindCutter, it is simply a matter of lifting the rod slowly, getting it quite high, and then, before the line can sink back again, proceed into whatever spey cast you are going to do. This works very well with the shorter sink tips. You should have no problem lifting a 15-foot, type-8 tip close enough to the surface to be able to spey cast easily. The secret to success is making sure you see half of the sink tip out of the water and then starting the spey cast while the sink tip is still visible and point P far away as possible. If you can't lift the line up high enough to see the tip (because the head is too long, the rod too short, or you haven't got the knack!), there is no point in starting the spey cast. You must be able to lift the line close enough to the surface for the cast to succeed.

Another way to cast sinking lines is to use the roll cast to bring the line up to the surface. The number of roll casts you'll need to make depends on how deep the line and fly have sunk. The longer sink tips (24 feet and more), full sinking lines, short spey rods, and the long-head interchangeable tip lines like the GrandSpey will all make roll casts necessary. Years ago I used to fish the river Spey in February and March. Because of the snowmelt, the river was always high and cold and to have any chance of catching a fish we used double-taper, 10-weight type-4, full-sinking lines. Coupled with big brass tube flies, these lines get down and would stay down. A single roll cast would never lift the fly up near enough to the surface to be able to start the spey cast, and it would take four or five very hard and powerful roll casts, in rapid succession, to get the fly

Another way to get a sinking line to the surface is to roll cast, but make enough roll casts to lift the fly clean out of the water. It may only take one roll cast, or it may take four to get the fly to lift out.

up and shallow enough to continue with a spey cast. That was hard work!

If you use full sinking lines, then these roll casts are the only way of getting the fly up toward the surface. I get lazier as time goes by and find that three or four hard roll casts before beginning a spey cast is more tiring than I like, and now I use sink tips for all my deep fishing. The availability of sink tips of different densities and interchangeable sink tips has completely changed the way I fish. I can put on a 24-foot, 400-grain Density Compensated Big Boy-type

If you are roll casting with a sinking line, ensure that the spey cast starts immediately when the fly lifts clear, otherwise the line will sink back down and everything must start again!

sink tip and keep the fly as deep as I ever did with the full sinking line. Most of the casting portion of the fly line is floating, so I need only a single roll cast to get the line up to the surface. Less work, more fishing time, more fish!

The final way to successfully cast sinking tip fly lines is to use a cast that has a powerful start to it. The snap T and the snake roll are great examples. In both cases the casts have enough power on the back-

stroke to lift the sink tip to the surface on its own—without the need for a roll cast or a high lift. Indeed, the snap T is the cast of choice for many West Coast steelheaders who use sink tip lines most of the time. If this is the option you choose, just remember not to pause too long between the snap and the chase; otherwise the sink tip will start to sink again.

The interchangeable tip spey line was developed in the United States by Jim Vincent and first manufactured by RIO Products. When steelhead fishing, he found that he frequently needed to change the depth of the line he was using, and rather than cut off the fly, wind in, change the spool and line, rethread the rod, and then start fishing again, he began experimenting with a loop-to-loop joining system. What he created was the interchangeable-tip fly line, basically a floating line, but with a loop-to-loop join 15 feet from the tip. This type of line comes with a wallet with various sinking tips. It is a simple matter to unthread the floating tip and thread in the sinking tip of the density you want to use. To get really deep, you can use a spey line with a second loop-to-loop joined 12 to 15 feet back from the first loops. You can buy 24- and 30-foot-long sinking tips and unloop both floating tips (30 feet in all), loop on the new long tip, and dredge! Alternatively, you can make your own sinking tips out of level, fast-sinking shooting-head material like lead core or T-14 and cut them to whatever length you need.

This interchangeable tip–type fly line is great for fishing. It means I can fish and travel light, with a wallet of four or five different tips in my pocket, and don't need to buy and carry extra lines, reels, and spools.

Whatever system you use, even if you still use full-sinking fly lines, remember to start the spey cast with either a good lift or a roll cast to get the line up to the surface. Keep roll casting until you see the fly pop out of the water and then immediately go into your spey cast. You do need to be quite skillful with your spey cast before you get serious with sinking lines. You don't have a moment of time between final roll cast and the start of the spey before the line sinks again, so you must be able to spey cast automatically, without thinking. Once the fly has popped out, if you panic who knows what cast will result!

With the longer sinking tips and full sinking lines, the roll cast is the only way to get the fly close enough to the surface to make a spey cast. Here the fly has swung to the dangle and is too deep to make a spey cast with.

The start of the roll cast begins to pull the fly toward the surface. Start the forward cast early, and with the point P well in front of you, so the line doesn't have a chance to sink.

As soon as you make the final roll cast, when the fly has lifted out of the water, start the spey cast while the line is still near the surface.

When using a shooting head to spey cast, you will be less likely to tear the anchor out of the water if you have some of the shooting line outside the rod tip.

SHOOTING HEADS

More and more spey casters are beginning to cast with shooting heads. There are advantages to using a shooting head—both in casting and in fishing. They are easy lines to cast, require little effort to get distance, and you can easily switch between the overhead cast and spey casting when using shooting heads. Certainly, with the overhead cast, shooting heads cannot be beaten for ease and distance. When you are spey casting with very little open area behind you and you can form only the smallest belly, it is much easier to get distance with the shooting head than it is with a regular spey line, particularly with the underand style of casting. (See chapter 16 for the underhand cast.)

The main advantage when fishing a shooting head is that the sinking heads get down and stay down. There is no drag on the thin shooting line to lift the head up when you're swinging through a pool and nothing to prevent it from sinking in the first place.

With this type of line you can change lines fast. If conditions change or you decide that something is not quite right and it is time to make a line change, you don't have to cut off the fly. Wind the line in, change reels or spools, and then restring the rod before tying the fly back on—an operation that, with these big rods, usually means wading ashore. With the shooting-head system, you can pull the line in, unloop the leader and hang it around your neck,

unloop the shooting head, loop in the new shooting head and then the leader, and start fishing again—no wading ashore and out of the bucket. It is fast, efficient, and catches more fish!

The downside of shooting heads is that you have to strip in line before each cast. You have a lot of line swirling around in the current, and you have to shoot it out again. Casters have developed elaborate ways of reducing the drag of all this shooting line while in mid-spey cast. I have seen casters coil up the line and then hold the coils in their mouth. I hope they remembered to open their mouths at the right time! Some casters use stripping baskets or line trays to hold the line and others cast from the bank, preferring to lay the shooting line on the ground. Many casters pull the shooting line in large coils and hold a single coil under each finger—opening their fingers at the right time to shoot the line effectively (and not drop the rod!). Another way around this is to pull in the shooting line in two or three very large coils and hang them from the index finger of the upper hand. This way works best for me, although it does produce the occasional tangle. Sometimes when you make a cast, the rod will rotate and one of the coils will bunch and tangle into another. You get a big cloggy bunch of line jammed in the butt ring with your line going nowhere.

The hardest thing for me to adjust to when I'm spey casting a shooting head is how short the line is and how easy it is to rip the anchor off the water. The casting stroke must be really shortened and the backcast placed gently into position. Any kick on the backcast results in losing the anchor point and a failed cast. One way around this is to have some of the shooting line outside the rod before you start the cast. The more skilled a caster you become, the longer the line can be. If you need to roll cast, remember that it is almost impossible to roll cast effectively with more than a few inches of shooting line outside the rod.

I rarely, if ever, use heads for spey casting. I prefer the longer-head lines that don't require stripping in and having to worry about coils. True, these longer-head lines take more effort and skill to cast, but I find that less of a problem than having to deal with loose running line as I make my cast.

CHAPTER 26

Leaders

Aspey casting leader is no different from any other type of leader. Its purpose is to assist the turnover of the line and to aid in the delicate presentation of the fly. The leader also effects the way the fly fishes, as well as the depth the fly fishes—particularly with the floating line.

FLOATING LINES

A good rule of thumb when choosing a leader is to relate it to the size of the fly. The bigger the fly (or the heavier), the thicker the leader needs to be to turn it over. If you're fishing in low-water conditions and with small flies, say size 12, use a tapered leader down to about 8 pounds. You need a fine leader for the lightweight fly to work in the light current. On the other hand, when you are fishing a 3-inch brass tube in high water you need a much, much heavier-handed approach. For this type of fishing, I would set up with 20 or 25 pounds of level monofil and keep it short—4 feet or so. This setup has little to do with the size of the fish you're after.

There are a number of good knotless tapered leaders on the market specially made for salmon or steelhead fishing. The monofil in these is usually made of a stiffer material than the lighter trout leaders because of the larger flies and heavier weights that need to be turned over. Lengths vary from 15 feet right down to 3-foot dredger leaders. For floating lines, a tapered leader is essential and can improve anybody's cast. If you prefer to tie your own tapered leaders, be prepared for a little work. To get the best

and most effective taper usually requires a leader to be made up of some seven or eight pieces of monofil, and few anglers I know like that kind of work. There is no one perfect leader design, as everyone casts differently, has different tackle set ups, and fishes different conditions with different fly sizes. I tie up three basic leader designs for floating-line fishing. My standard late spring, early summer, early autumn leader for fishing and spey casting is 11 feet long and tapered down to a 13.2-pound point. In the colder months I usually fish with bigger flies and a leader of 8 feet and tapered to 17.6 pounds. Finally, in the summer months, for low water and size 10 and 12 flies, I use a leader of 14 feet with a tippet of 8 or 10 pounds. These are the leaders that have served me well and work for me. You may not get on with them and need to adjust accordingly. Here are the taper design and section lengths of the leaders I prefer.

8 feet tapered to 17.6 pounds. This is a fairly simple leader to tie up. Since I am fishing the heavier flies with this leader, I usually use a stiff material throughout, such as a hard saltwater monofil. I start with 2 feet of 33 pounds (0.0265 inches), tied to 22 inches of 26 pounds (0.024 inches), to 14 inches of 22 pounds (0.022 inches), and finally a level 3-foot tippet of 17.6 pounds (0.019 inches).

11 feet tapered to 13.2 pounds. With this leader I like a little more movement in the fly and tend

followed and the loop tries to fire in a different direction from the target, resulting in a collision.

creep. When the caster slightly anticipates the forward stroke by creeping the rod forward before the forward cast should start. This causes a shortening of the forward stroke, which results in little power and a poor forward cast.

crude spey. The very first single spey. Still useful today when there is absolutely no space to backcast.

crumpled anchor. An anchor that lies on the water in a slack heap instead of straight and taut. Also known as the piled anchor.

D loop. Another term for the belly.

dangle. When the fly line has swung around in the current as far as it will go and lies taut and motionless directly downstream of you.

deadline roll cast. The basic roll cast where the belly is small and hangs lifelessly as the forward cast starts.

devon switch. A cast that changes direction with no anchor or line stick; basically, an airborne single spey.

double anchor point. Usually associated with the double spey, where the fly lands slightly upstream of the caster on stage 1. A good reaction from the caster can pull this anchor point around to the downstream side with the right move to make the cast safe.

double spey. A change of direction cast with a limited backcast. Performed with the downstream arm and used when there is no wind or a downstream wind.

double taper. A fly line that has an identical taper at each end and a level body section.

downstream wind. A wind that blows downstream with the current.

dreaded dip. To keep tension in the line on backcasts, the rod should travel in a straight line, slightly rising. A dip put into the cast causes momentum to be lost and results in a bloody L. A common error in spey casting.

drift. When the rod drifts back at the end of the backstroke while the rear loop is traveling back. This gives the caster a longer forward stroke, greater acceleration, higher line speed, and more distance.

drift lift. When the rod drifts sideways as the initial lift starts instead of lifting vertically. A common error in spey casting usually associated with the single spey.

dry fly spey. A spey cast used with the single-handed rod when fishing with a dry fly and trying to avoid getting the fly wet.

energy ratio. The relationship between the size and energy of the belly and the amount of power the forward cast needs. The bigger the belly, the less forward power is needed.

forward spey. Another term for the switch cast.

grass leader. A leader designed for spey casting on grass. Made like barbed wire with stiff mono and long tags to grip the grass.

grip. Another term for the anchor.

hang down. Another term for the dangle.

haul. Where the free hand (with a single-handed rod) pulls the line to give it more line speed during a backcast or forward stroke.

head. The front part of the fly line that includes the front taper, the body, and the back taper.

hook. When you swing the rod too far around behind your head on the backstroke and pull the belly and rod tip away from the 180-degree plane.

in leg. Where the rod kicks back and in toward your bank on stage 2 of the advanced double spey.

jump roll. Another term for the switch cast.

kiss. When the line tip lightly brushes the water before the forward cast starts. Only applicable with the splash-and-go group of casts.

late tilt. A perfect forward cast starts by driving the rod forward while keeping the rod pointed back. At the last moment, the rod tilts and fires the forward stroke out.

left bank. The side of the river on the left as you look downstream.

level drop. When the line drops horizontally on the backcast of a single spey, snake roll, or switch cast. Results in either no anchor going forward before any line lands or too much stick as the line lands all at once. A common error in spey casting.

line stick. The second basic principle. Refers to the amount of line lying on the water surface as the forward cast starts. The more line on the water, the more energy is lost in the forward cast and the worse the result. Also called anchor.

lines of energy. When the forward cast and backcast are in complete alignment with no change of plane as the forward cast drives out.

live line roll. Another term for the switch cast. The belly is large, has energy, and loads the rod easily.

long belly. A fly line that has a long head. In spey casting terms, this is usually over 70 feet.

mending. A curve deliberately thrown into the line to change the way the fly fishes on the swing.

modern spey. Casting using flatter rod movements and faster-action rods.

needle-pointed loop. A really tight loop with a very sharp point. The finest and most efficient shape for a loop.

180-degree principle. The third basic principle. The most efficient cast has all factors controlling the cast in alignment. The belly, the line stick, and the rod are all lined up for an easy efficient cast to the target.

oozlum spey. A spey cast useless for fishing that is nonetheless fun to learn and a great way to practice line control.

orange line. An imaginary line that you picture directly between your front foot and the final target.

out leg. When the rod kicks out toward the river on stage 2 of the advanced double spey.

passive belly. A belly that has no momentum other than its own weight to load the rod at the start of the forward cast.

perry poke. A type of spey cast that can really help load the rod. A substitute for the single spey.

piled anchor. When the anchor lies on the water in a pile of slack line, not straight and taut. Also called crumpled anchor.

pirouette. When stage 2 is made at the correct speed and height, the white mouse runs all the way to the fly line tip and the fly line pirouettes right on the nail knot. The entire fly line changes position and aligns with the target. Relevant to the double spey and snap T.

point P. The exact spot where the belly touches the water surface at the end of the backstroke.

reverse bloody L. A bloody L that is bent downstream rather than upstream on the single spey

or snap T. Usually caused by not getting the fly to land upstream of the orange line after the backstroke.

right bank. The side of the river on the right as you look downstream.

river left. Another term for the left bank of the river.

river right. Another term for the right bank of the river.

roll cast. The basic spey cast. A cast with virtually no backcast, no change of direction, and limited distance possibilities.

shooting head. A short line used for spey and overhead casting. Attached to a thin shooting line and good for distance.

shooting line. The thin line that a shooting head is attached to that helps get distance and depth.

side spey. A spey cast with the single-handed rod where the forward loop travels out on a side plane. Useful for getting underneath an overhanging tree.

single spey. A change of direction cast with no backcast, performed with the upstream arm and used when there is no wind or an upstream wind.

sliding or slithering anchor. Achieved at the end of stage 2 when the nail knot doesn't just pirouette, but slides slightly back directly away from the target. The best anchor to get on the double spey or snap T, it is very hard to master.

snake roll. A change of direction cast with a limited backcast, performed with the downstream arm and used when there is no wind or a downstream wind. A faster change of direction cast than the double spey.

snap C. A change of direction cast with a limited backcast, performed with the upstream arm and used when there is no wind or an upstream wind. A much easier cast to learn than the single spey.

snap T. A change of direction cast with a limited backcast, performed with the upstream arm and used when there is no wind or an upstream wind. Much easier cast to learn than the single spey.

spey. A style of casting used when there is limited or no backcasting room. A back loop is formed below the rod tip and connected from the rod tip to an anchor point in the water. Usually used with a change of direction on the forward cast.

spey rod. A term commonly used in the United States for a two-handed fly rod.

spey taper. A modern fly line designed to make spey casting with a two-handed rod easier. Lengths and tapers vary considerably, but all spey taper lines are much heavier than their single-handed counterparts.

spiral spey. A form of the single spey where the rod draws a C shape prior to the backstroke to cleanly break the surface film and make it easier to position the anchor. Ideally suited for casting long lengths of double taper or long belly spey line.

splash and go group. A group of casts that have an airborne backcast and instantaneous forward stroke, which begins as soon as the line tip touches the water at the end of the backcast.

stick. The second basic principle. Refers to the amount of line lying on the water surface as the forward cast starts. The more line on the water, the more energy is lost in the forward cast and the worse the result. Also known as anchor.

switch cast. A more advanced form of the roll cast with a limited backcast and no change of direction but great distances possible.

tailing loop. When the forward loop unrolls, crossing and catching itself. Caused by either the rod moving too sharply and suddenly on the forward stroke or breaking the 180-degree plane.

traditional spey. Traditional style of casting with more rounded rod movements and lifts and dips with softer action salmon rods.

trunk. When the bottom hand gripping the rod lifts on the backcast, making the rod tip drop and creating too much stick. A common error in spey casting.

turbo spey. A spey cast used with a single-handed rod that increases line speed and distance by adding a single or double haul.

two-handed rod. A rod with extra long cork grips, designed to be cast with two hands.

underhand casting. A form of spey casting using shooting heads, developed and mastered in Sweden by Goran Anderson.

upstream wind. A wind that blows upstream against the current.

V loop. An advanced belly, not rounded, more pointed and wedge shaped.

waterborne anchor group. A group of casts that does not have an airborne backcast but relies on the point when the belly, or D loop, stops to judge the right time to start the forward cast.

wedge-shaped loop. A loop that is not rounded but pointed like an arrowhead.

white mouse. The spray caused by the fly line tearing out of the water on stage 2 of the double spey or snap T.

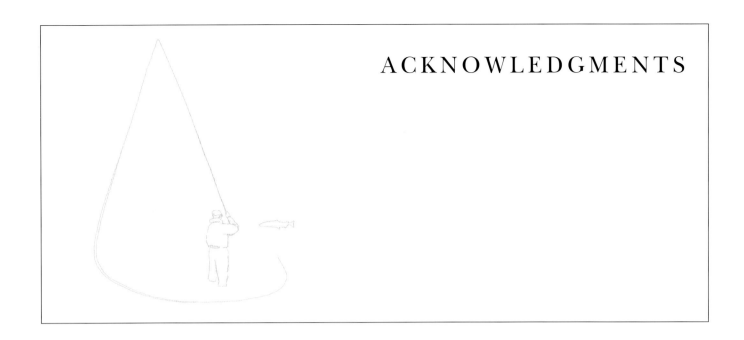

ACKNOWLEDGMENTS

The world of spey casting is constantly changing and new casts, techniques, tackle, and, more importantly to me, newer and better ways of teaching casting have been developed. As I have been working on this book for many years, I have started it, put it off, started it again, written and rewritten, and eventually finished it. That the book ever got finished is due to the encouragement, enthusiasm, and commitment of my wife, Susan.

There are many people that I need to thank for their help. Susan is at the top of the list, as she is with everything in my life. She proofread the manuscript, corrected my grammar and tenses and made the techno-babble more understandable. Without her help, this book would read like a computer manual!

For my interest and knowledge in fly casting, I thank my father, John Gawesworth. He taught me the skills and kindled my passion for spey casting and showed me how to teach casting in clear and concise ways. Without my dad, I would not have found such an enjoyable way of making a living. He's a great man and a great instructor.

There are hundreds of other people that have helped me with my spey casting and with this book. Greg Pearson and Scott Nelson are skilled in illustrating and photography, respectively, and without their mastery of the arts, this book would be the poorer. A great big thanks to Judith Schnell at Stackpole Books for having faith in me and all the great help in putting the book together and to Jay Nichols for introducing us. Thanks to Tom McGuane for giving me the idea and confidence to start this project all those years ago in Tierra del Fuego. A big thank you to Tom Dorsey at Thomas & Thomas for making on a week's notice the white rod used in the photographs. For their technical help, I want like to thank Tom Dorsey, Lon Deckard, and Trevor Bross at Thomas & Thomas; John Middleton, Steve McCaveney, Nobuo Nodera, and David Bell at Daiwa Sports; Shannon Robinson, Ryan Harrison, and Mark Farriss at Waterworks Lamson; Paul Johnson, Mark Bale, and Jerry Siem at Sage; Egan Anderson at Scott Fly Rods; and Jim Vincent, Marlin Roush, and John Harder at RIO Products. I know a number of you have moved on from these companies, but you were there when you helped me with the book.

Thanks also to Hans Terje Anonsen, Alan Williams, Jan Sjaastad, Mark Birbeck, Bo Ivanovic, Dru Montague, David Hoare, Derek and Peter Kyte, and all at Frontiers Travel for their kind invitations to visit and fish some of the most wonderful riverbanks on earth.

Thanks to the great spey casters of the world who have supported, challenged, demonstrated, and taught me more about spey casting than I could have ever picked up on my own. In Europe: Gary Coxon, Ally Gowans, Leif Stavmo, Michael Evans, Stephen Peterson, Derek Brown, Eoin Fairgrieve,

Andy Murray, and numerous Scottish ghillies. In North America: Jim Vincent, Mike and Denise Maxwell, Dec Hogan, Ed Ward, Steve Choate, Way Yin, Dana Sturn, Scott O'Donnell, Mike McClure, John and Amy Hazel, Mel Kreiger, Al Buhr, Brian Silvey, and Tim Rajeff. In the rest of the world: Nobuo Nodera, a superb spey caster from Japan, and Max Manamaev, one of the finest guides I have had the pleasure to work with and an unbelievably good spey caster from Russia. I have not yet cast with the other greats in the world of spey casting, though I eagerly anticipate these meetings.

Finally, I must thank all the students who have paid me to do something I so enjoy—teaching casting. I owe so much to you all.

I know I have left out some people and I am sorry for that. This book is the result of what I have learned from others and all of you should be named. If your name is not here, it isn't because I didn't value your help, it's that my tired old brain forgets!

INDEX

Italic page numbers refer to illustrations.